Sage Tutorial

Release 6.1.1

The Sage Development Team

May 28, 2014

CONTENTS

1 Introduction — 3
    1.1 Installation — 4
    1.2 Ways to Use Sage — 4
    1.3 Longterm Goals for Sage — 5

2 A Guided Tour — 7
    2.1 Assignment, Equality, and Arithmetic — 7
    2.2 Getting Help — 9
    2.3 Functions, Indentation, and Counting — 11
    2.4 Basic Algebra and Calculus — 14
    2.5 Plotting — 20
    2.6 Some Common Issues with Functions — 23
    2.7 Basic Rings — 26
    2.8 Linear Algebra — 29
    2.9 Polynomials — 32
    2.10 Parents, Conversion and Coercion — 37
    2.11 Finite Groups, Abelian Groups — 42
    2.12 Number Theory — 44
    2.13 Some More Advanced Mathematics — 46

3 The Interactive Shell — 55
    3.1 Your Sage Session — 55
    3.2 Logging Input and Output — 57
    3.3 Paste Ignores Prompts — 58
    3.4 Timing Commands — 58
    3.5 Other IPython tricks — 60
    3.6 Errors and Exceptions — 61
    3.7 Reverse Search and Tab Completion — 62
    3.8 Integrated Help System — 63
    3.9 Saving and Loading Individual Objects — 65
    3.10 Saving and Loading Complete Sessions — 67
    3.11 The Notebook Interface — 68

4 Interfaces — 71
- 4.1 GP/PARI — 71
- 4.2 GAP — 73
- 4.3 Singular — 73
- 4.4 Maxima — 74

5 Sage, LaTeX and Friends — 77
- 5.1 Overview — 77
- 5.2 Basic Use — 78
- 5.3 Customizing LaTeX Generation — 79
- 5.4 Customizing LaTeX Processing — 81
- 5.5 An Example: Combinatorial Graphs with tkz-graph — 83
- 5.6 A Fully Capable TeX Installation — 84
- 5.7 External Programs — 84

6 Programming — 85
- 6.1 Loading and Attaching Sage files — 85
- 6.2 Creating Compiled Code — 86
- 6.3 Standalone Python/Sage Scripts — 87
- 6.4 Data Types — 88
- 6.5 Lists, Tuples, and Sequences — 89
- 6.6 Dictionaries — 91
- 6.7 Sets — 92
- 6.8 Iterators — 93
- 6.9 Loops, Functions, Control Statements, and Comparisons — 93
- 6.10 Profiling — 96

7 Using SageTeX — 99

8 Afterword — 101
- 8.1 Why Python? — 101
- 8.2 I would like to contribute somehow. How can I? — 103
- 8.3 How do I reference Sage? — 103

9 Appendix — 105
- 9.1 Arithmetical binary operator precedence — 105

10 Bibliography — 107

11 Indices and tables — 109

Bibliography — 111

Sage Tutorial, Release 6.1.1

Sage is free, open-source math software that supports research and teaching in algebra, geometry, number theory, cryptography, numerical computation, and related areas. Both the Sage development model and the technology in Sage itself are distinguished by an extremely strong emphasis on openness, community, cooperation, and collaboration: we are building the car, not reinventing the wheel. The overall goal of Sage is to create a viable, free, open-source alternative to Maple, Mathematica, Magma, and MATLAB.

This tutorial is the best way to become familiar with Sage in only a few hours. You can read it in HTML or PDF versions, or from the Sage notebook (click `Help`, then click `Tutorial` to interactively work through the tutorial from within Sage).

This work is licensed under a Creative Commons Attribution-Share Alike 3.0 License.

CHAPTER
ONE

INTRODUCTION

This tutorial should take at most 3-4 hours to fully work through. You can read it in HTML or PDF versions, or from the Sage notebook click `Help`, then click `Tutorial` to interactively work through the tutorial from within Sage.

Though much of Sage is implemented using Python, no Python background is needed to read this tutorial. You will want to learn Python (a very fun language!) at some point, and there are many excellent free resources for doing so including [PyT] and [Dive]. If you just want to quickly try out Sage, this tutorial is the place to start. For example:

```
sage: 2 + 2
4
sage: factor(-2007)
-1 * 3^2 * 223

sage: A = matrix(4,4, range(16)); A
[ 0  1  2  3]
[ 4  5  6  7]
[ 8  9 10 11]
[12 13 14 15]

sage: factor(A.charpoly())
x^2 * (x^2 - 30*x - 80)

sage: m = matrix(ZZ,2, range(4))
sage: m[0,0] = m[0,0] - 3
sage: m
[-3  1]
[ 2  3]

sage: E = EllipticCurve([1,2,3,4,5]);
sage: E
Elliptic Curve defined by y^2 + x*y + 3*y = x^3 + 2*x^2 + 4*x + 5
over Rational Field
sage: E.anlist(10)
[0, 1, 1, 0, -1, -3, 0, -1, -3, -3, -3]
sage: E.rank()
1
```

3

```
sage: k = 1/(sqrt(3)*I + 3/4 + sqrt(73)*5/9); k
36/(20*sqrt(73) + 36*I*sqrt(3) + 27)
sage: N(k)
0.165495678130644 - 0.0521492082074256*I
sage: N(k,30)      # 30 "bits"
0.16549568 - 0.052149208*I
sage: latex(k)
\frac{36}{20 \, \sqrt{73} + 36 i \, \sqrt{3} + 27}
```

1.1 Installation

If you do not have Sage installed on a computer and just want to try some commands, use online at http://www.sagenb.org.

See the Sage Installation Guide in the documentation section of the main Sage webpage [SA] for instructions on installing Sage on your computer. Here we merely make a few comments.

1. The Sage download file comes with "batteries included". In other words, although Sage uses Python, IPython, PARI, GAP, Singular, Maxima, NTL, GMP, and so on, you do not need to install them separately as they are included with the Sage distribution. However, to use certain Sage features, e.g., Macaulay or KASH, you must install the relevant optional package or at least have the relevant programs installed on your computer already. Macaulay and KASH are Sage packages (for a list of available optional packages, type `sage -optional`, or browse the "Download" page on the Sage website).

2. The pre-compiled binary version of Sage (found on the Sage web site) may be easier and quicker to install than the source code version. Just unpack the file and run `sage`.

3. If you'd like to use the SageTeX package (which allows you to embed the results of Sage computations into a LaTeX file), you will need to make SageTeX known to your TeX distribution. To do this, see the section "Make SageTeX known to TeX" in the Sage installation guide (this link should take you to a local copy of the installation guide). It's quite easy; you just need to set an environment variable or copy a single file to a directory that TeX will search.

    The documentation for using SageTeX is located in
    `$SAGE_ROOT/local/share/texmf/tex/generic/sagetex/`, where "$SAGE_ROOT" refers to the directory where you installed Sage – for example, `/opt/sage-4.2.1`.

1.2 Ways to Use Sage

You can use Sage in several ways.

- **Notebook graphical interface:** see the section on the Notebook in the reference manual and *The Notebook Interface* below,

- **Interactive command line:** see *The Interactive Shell*,

- **Programs:** By writing interpreted and compiled programs in Sage (see *Loading and Attaching Sage files* and *Creating Compiled Code*), and
- **Scripts:** by writing stand-alone Python scripts that use the Sage library (see *Standalone Python/Sage Scripts*).

1.3 Longterm Goals for Sage

- **Useful**: Sage's intended audience is mathematics students (from high school to graduate school), teachers, and research mathematicians. The aim is to provide software that can be used to explore and experiment with mathematical constructions in algebra, geometry, number theory, calculus, numerical computation, etc. Sage helps make it easier to interactively experiment with mathematical objects.
- **Efficient:** Be fast. Sage uses highly-optimized mature software like GMP, PARI, GAP, and NTL, and so is very fast at certain operations.
- **Free and open source:** The source code must be freely available and readable, so users can understand what the system is really doing and more easily extend it. Just as mathematicians gain a deeper understanding of a theorem by carefully reading or at least skimming the proof, people who do computations should be able to understand how the calculations work by reading documented source code. If you use Sage to do computations in a paper you publish, you can rest assured that your readers will always have free access to Sage and all its source code, and you are even allowed to archive and re-distribute the version of Sage you used.
- **Easy to compile:** Sage should be easy to compile from source for Linux, OS X and Windows users. This provides more flexibility for users to modify the system.
- **Cooperation:** Provide robust interfaces to most other computer algebra systems, including PARI, GAP, Singular, Maxima, KASH, Magma, Maple, and Mathematica. Sage is meant to unify and extend existing math software.
- **Well documented:** Tutorial, programming guide, reference manual, and how-to, with numerous examples and discussion of background mathematics.
- **Extensible:** Be able to define new data types or derive from built-in types, and use code written in a range of languages.
- **User friendly**: It should be easy to understand what functionality is provided for a given object and to view documentation and source code. Also attain a high level of user support.

CHAPTER
TWO

A GUIDED TOUR

This section is a guided tour of some of what is available in Sage. For many more examples, see "Sage Constructions", which is intended to answer the general question "How do I construct ...?". See also the "Sage Reference Manual", which has thousands more examples. Also note that you can interactively work through this tour in the Sage notebook by clicking the `Help` link.

(If you are viewing the tutorial in the Sage notebook, press `shift-enter` to evaluate any input cell. You can even edit the input before pressing shift-enter. On some Macs you might have to press `shift-return` rather than `shift-enter`.)

2.1 Assignment, Equality, and Arithmetic

With some minor exceptions, Sage uses the Python programming language, so most introductory books on Python will help you to learn Sage.

Sage uses = for assignment. It uses ==, <=, >=, < and > for comparison:

```
sage: a = 5
sage: a
5
sage: 2 == 2
True
sage: 2 == 3
False
sage: 2 < 3
True
sage: a == 5
True
```

Sage provides all of the basic mathematical operations:

```
sage: 2**3    #  ** means exponent
8
sage: 2^3     #  ^ is a synonym for ** (unlike in Python)
8
sage: 10 % 3  #  for integer arguments, % means mod, i.e., remainder
1
```

7

```
sage: 10/4
5/2
sage: 10//4    # for integer arguments, // returns the integer quotient
2
sage: 4 * (10 // 4) + 10 % 4 == 10
True
sage: 3^2*4 + 2%5
38
```

The computation of an expression like `3^2*4 + 2%5` depends on the order in which the operations are applied; this is specified in the "operator precedence table" in *Arithmetical binary operator precedence*.

Sage also provides many familiar mathematical functions; here are just a few examples:

```
sage: sqrt(3.4)
1.84390889145858
sage: sin(5.135)
-0.912021158525540
sage: sin(pi/3)
1/2*sqrt(3)
```

As the last example shows, some mathematical expressions return 'exact' values, rather than numerical approximations. To get a numerical approximation, use either the function `n` or the method `n` (and both of these have a longer name, `numerical_approx`, and the function `N` is the same as `n`)). These take optional arguments `prec`, which is the requested number of bits of precision, and `digits`, which is the requested number of decimal digits of precision; the default is 53 bits of precision.

```
sage: exp(2)
e^2
sage: n(exp(2))
7.38905609893065
sage: sqrt(pi).numerical_approx()
1.77245385090552
sage: sin(10).n(digits=5)
-0.54402
sage: N(sin(10),digits=10)
-0.5440211109
sage: numerical_approx(pi, prec=200)
3.1415926535897932384626433832795028841971693993751058209749
```

Python is dynamically typed, so the value referred to by each variable has a type associated with it, but a given variable may hold values of any Python type within a given scope:

```
sage: a = 5    # a is an integer
sage: type(a)
<type 'sage.rings.integer.Integer'>
sage: a = 5/3  # now a is a rational number
sage: type(a)
<type 'sage.rings.rational.Rational'>
sage: a = 'hello'  # now a is a string
sage: type(a)
<type 'str'>
```

The C programming language, which is statically typed, is much different; a variable declared to hold an int can only hold an int in its scope.

A potential source of confusion in Python is that an integer literal that begins with a zero is treated as an octal number, i.e., a number in base 8.

```
sage: 011
9
sage: 8 + 1
9
sage: n = 011
sage: n.str(8)    # string representation of n in base 8
'11'
```

This is consistent with the C programming language.

2.2 Getting Help

Sage has extensive built-in documentation, accessible by typing the name of a function or a constant (for example), followed by a question mark:

```
sage: tan?
Type:        <class 'sage.calculus.calculus.Function_tan'>
Definition:  tan( [noargspec] )
Docstring:

    The tangent function

    EXAMPLES:
        sage: tan(pi)
        0
        sage: tan(3.1415)
        -0.0000926535900581913
        sage: tan(3.1415/4)
        0.999953674278156
        sage: tan(pi/4)
        1
        sage: tan(1/2)
        tan(1/2)
        sage: RR(tan(1/2))
        0.546302489843790
sage: log2?
Type:        <class 'sage.functions.constants.Log2'>
Definition:  log2( [noargspec] )
Docstring:

    The natural logarithm of the real number 2.

    EXAMPLES:
        sage: log2
        log2
```

```
        sage: float(log2)
        0.69314718055994529
        sage: RR(log2)
        0.693147180559945
        sage: R = RealField(200); R
        Real Field with 200 bits of precision
        sage: R(log2)
        0.69314718055994530941723212145817656807550013436025525412068
        sage: l = (1-log2)/(1+log2); l
        (1 - log(2))/(log(2) + 1)
        sage: R(l)
        0.18123221829928249948761381864650311423330609774776013488056
        sage: maxima(log2)
        log(2)
        sage: maxima(log2).float()
        .6931471805599453
        sage: gp(log2)
        0.6931471805599453094172321215              # 32-bit
        0.69314718055994530941723212145817656807    # 64-bit
sage: sudoku?
File:           sage/local/lib/python2.5/site-packages/sage/games/sudoku.py
Type:           <type 'function'>
Definition:     sudoku(A)
Docstring:

    Solve the 9x9 Sudoku puzzle defined by the matrix A.

    EXAMPLE:
        sage: A = matrix(ZZ,9,[5,0,0, 0,8,0, 0,4,9, 0,0,0, 5,0,0,
    0,3,0, 0,6,7, 3,0,0, 0,0,1, 1,5,0, 0,0,0, 0,0,0, 0,0,0, 2,0,8, 0,0,0,
    0,0,0, 0,0,0, 0,1,8, 7,0,0, 0,0,4, 1,5,0,    0,3,0, 0,0,2,
    0,0,0, 4,9,0, 0,5,0, 0,0,3])
        sage: A
        [5 0 0 0 8 0 0 4 9]
        [0 0 0 5 0 0 0 3 0]
        [0 6 7 3 0 0 0 0 1]
        [1 5 0 0 0 0 0 0 0]
        [0 0 0 2 0 8 0 0 0]
        [0 0 0 0 0 0 0 1 8]
        [7 0 0 0 0 4 1 5 0]
        [0 3 0 0 0 2 0 0 0]
        [4 9 0 0 5 0 0 0 3]
        sage: sudoku(A)
        [5 1 3 6 8 7 2 4 9]
        [8 4 9 5 2 1 6 3 7]
        [2 6 7 3 4 9 5 8 1]
        [1 5 8 4 6 3 9 7 2]
        [9 7 4 2 1 8 3 6 5]
        [3 2 6 7 9 5 4 1 8]
        [7 8 2 9 3 4 1 5 6]
        [6 3 5 1 7 2 8 9 4]
        [4 9 1 8 5 6 7 2 3]
```

Sage also provides 'Tab completion': type the first few letters of a function and then hit the tab key. For example, if you type `ta` followed by `TAB`, Sage will print `tachyon, tan, tanh, taylor`. This provides a good way to find the names of functions and other structures in Sage.

2.3 Functions, Indentation, and Counting

To define a new function in Sage, use the `def` command and a colon after the list of variable names. For example:

```
sage: def is_even(n):
...       return n%2 == 0
...
sage: is_even(2)
True
sage: is_even(3)
False
```

Note: Depending on which version of the tutorial you are viewing, you may see three dots ... on the second line of this example. Do not type them; they are just to emphasize that the code is indented. Whenever this is the case, press [Return/Enter] once at the end of the block to insert a blank line and conclude the function definition.

You do not specify the types of any of the input arguments. You can specify multiple inputs, each of which may have an optional default value. For example, the function below defaults to `divisor=2` if `divisor` is not specified.

```
sage: def is_divisible_by(number, divisor=2):
...       return number%divisor == 0
sage: is_divisible_by(6,2)
True
sage: is_divisible_by(6)
True
sage: is_divisible_by(6, 5)
False
```

You can also explicitly specify one or either of the inputs when calling the function; if you specify the inputs explicitly, you can give them in any order:

```
sage: is_divisible_by(6, divisor=5)
False
sage: is_divisible_by(divisor=2, number=6)
True
```

In Python, blocks of code are not indicated by curly braces or begin and end blocks as in many other languages. Instead, blocks of code are indicated by indentation, which must match up exactly. For example, the following is a syntax error because the `return` statement is not indented the same amount as the other lines above it.

```
sage: def even(n):
...       v = []
...       for i in range(3,n):
```

```
...                if i % 2 == 0:
...                    v.append(i)
...        return v
Syntax Error:
       return v
```

If you fix the indentation, the function works:

```
sage: def even(n):
...        v = []
...        for i in range(3,n):
...            if i % 2 == 0:
...                v.append(i)
...        return v
sage: even(10)
[4, 6, 8]
```

Semicolons are not needed at the ends of lines; a line is in most cases ended by a newline. However, you can put multiple statements on one line, separated by semicolons:

```
sage: a = 5; b = a + 3; c = b^2; c
64
```

If you would like a single line of code to span multiple lines, use a terminating backslash:

```
sage: 2 + \
...     3
5
```

In Sage, you count by iterating over a range of integers. For example, the first line below is exactly like `for(i=0; i<3; i++)` in C++ or Java:

```
sage: for i in range(3):
...       print i
0
1
2
```

The first line below is like `for(i=2;i<5;i++)`.

```
sage: for i in range(2,5):
...       print i
2
3
4
```

The third argument controls the step, so the following is like `for(i=1;i<6;i+=2)`.

```
sage: for i in range(1,6,2):
...       print i
1
3
5
```

Often you will want to create a nice table to display numbers you have computed using Sage. One easy way to do this is to use string formatting. Below, we create three columns each of width exactly 6 and make a table of squares and cubes.

```
sage: for i in range(5):
...       print '%6s %6s %6s'%(i, i^2, i^3)
     0      0      0
     1      1      1
     2      4      8
     3      9     27
     4     16     64
```

The most basic data structure in Sage is the list, which is – as the name suggests – just a list of arbitrary objects. For example, the `range` command that we used creates a list:

```
sage: range(2,10)
[2, 3, 4, 5, 6, 7, 8, 9]
```

Here is a more complicated list:

```
sage: v = [1, "hello", 2/3, sin(x^3)]
sage: v
[1, 'hello', 2/3, sin(x^3)]
```

List indexing is 0-based, as in many programming languages.

```
sage: v[0]
1
sage: v[3]
sin(x^3)
```

Use `len(v)` to get the length of v, use `v.append(obj)` to append a new object to the end of v, and use `del v[i]` to delete the ith entry of v:

```
sage: len(v)
4
sage: v.append(1.5)
sage: v
[1, 'hello', 2/3, sin(x^3), 1.50000000000000]
sage: del v[1]
sage: v
[1, 2/3, sin(x^3), 1.50000000000000]
```

Another important data structure is the dictionary (or associative array). This works like a list, except that it can be indexed with almost any object (the indices must be immutable):

```
sage: d = {'hi':-2,  3/8:pi,   e:pi}
sage: d['hi']
-2
sage: d[e]
pi
```

You can also define new data types using classes. Encapsulating mathematical objects with classes is a powerful technique that can help to simplify and organize your Sage programs. Below, we define a class that

2.3. Functions, Indentation, and Counting

represents the list of even positive integers up to *n*; it derives from the builtin type `list`.

```
sage: class Evens(list):
...       def __init__(self, n):
...           self.n = n
...           list.__init__(self, range(2, n+1, 2))
...       def __repr__(self):
...           return "Even positive numbers up to n."
```

The `__init__` method is called to initialize the object when it is created; the `__repr__` method prints the object out. We call the list constructor method in the second line of the `__init__` method. We create an object of class `Evens` as follows:

```
sage: e = Evens(10)
sage: e
Even positive numbers up to n.
```

Note that `e` prints using the `__repr__` method that we defined. To see the underlying list of numbers, use the `list` function:

```
sage: list(e)
[2, 4, 6, 8, 10]
```

We can also access the `n` attribute or treat `e` like a list.

```
sage: e.n
10
sage: e[2]
6
```

2.4 Basic Algebra and Calculus

Sage can perform various computations related to basic algebra and calculus: for example, finding solutions to equations, differentiation, integration, and Laplace transforms. See the Sage Constructions documentation for more examples.

2.4.1 Solving Equations

Solving Equations Exactly

The `solve` function solves equations. To use it, first specify some variables; then the arguments to `solve` are an equation (or a system of equations), together with the variables for which to solve:

```
sage: x = var('x')
sage: solve(x^2 + 3*x + 2, x)
[x == -2, x == -1]
```

You can solve equations for one variable in terms of others:

```
sage: x, b, c = var('x b c')
sage: solve([x^2 + b*x + c == 0],x)
[x == -1/2*b - 1/2*sqrt(b^2 - 4*c), x == -1/2*b + 1/2*sqrt(b^2 - 4*c)]
```

You can also solve for several variables:

```
sage: x, y = var('x, y')
sage: solve([x+y==6, x-y==4], x, y)
[[x == 5, y == 1]]
```

The following example of using Sage to solve a system of non-linear equations was provided by Jason Grout: first, we solve the system symbolically:

```
sage: var('x y p q')
(x, y, p, q)
sage: eq1 = p+q==9
sage: eq2 = q*y+p*x==-6
sage: eq3 = q*y^2+p*x^2==24
sage: solve([eq1,eq2,eq3,p==1],p,q,x,y)
[[p == 1, q == 8, x == -4/3*sqrt(10) - 2/3, y == 1/6*sqrt(5)*sqrt(2) - 2/3],
 [p == 1, q == 8, x == 4/3*sqrt(10) - 2/3, y == -1/6*sqrt(5)*sqrt(2) - 2/3]]
```

For numerical approximations of the solutions, you can instead use:

```
sage: solns = solve([eq1,eq2,eq3,p==1],p,q,x,y, solution_dict=True)
sage: [[s[p].n(30), s[q].n(30), s[x].n(30), s[y].n(30)] for s in solns]
[[1.0000000, 8.0000000, -4.8830369, -0.13962039],
 [1.0000000, 8.0000000, 3.5497035, -1.1937129]]
```

(The function n prints a numerical approximation, and the argument is the number of bits of precision.)

Solving Equations Numerically

Often times, solve will not be able to find an exact solution to the equation or equations specified. When it fails, you can use find_root to find a numerical solution. For example, solve does not return anything interesting for the following equation:

```
sage: theta = var('theta')
sage: solve(cos(theta)==sin(theta), theta)
[sin(theta) == cos(theta)]
```

On the other hand, we can use find_root to find a solution to the above equation in the range $0 < \phi < \pi/2$:

```
sage: phi = var('phi')
sage: find_root(cos(phi)==sin(phi),0,pi/2)
0.785398163397448...
```

2.4.2 Differentiation, Integration, etc.

Sage knows how to differentiate and integrate many functions. For example, to differentiate $\sin(u)$ with respect to u, do the following:

```
sage: u = var('u')
sage: diff(sin(u), u)
cos(u)
```

To compute the fourth derivative of $\sin(x^2)$:

```
sage: diff(sin(x^2), x, 4)
16*x^4*sin(x^2) - 48*x^2*cos(x^2) - 12*sin(x^2)
```

To compute the partial derivatives of $x^2 + 17y^2$ with respect to x and y, respectively:

```
sage: x, y = var('x,y')
sage: f = x^2 + 17*y^2
sage: f.diff(x)
2*x
sage: f.diff(y)
34*y
```

We move on to integrals, both indefinite and definite. To compute $\int x \sin(x^2)\,dx$ and $\int_0^1 \frac{x}{x^2+1}\,dx$:

```
sage: integral(x*sin(x^2), x)
-1/2*cos(x^2)
sage: integral(x/(x^2+1), x, 0, 1)
1/2*log(2)
```

To compute the partial fraction decomposition of $\frac{1}{x^2-1}$:

```
sage: f = 1/((1+x)*(x-1))
sage: f.partial_fraction(x)
-1/2/(x + 1) + 1/2/(x - 1)
```

2.4.3 Solving Differential Equations

You can use Sage to investigate ordinary differential equations. To solve the equation $x' + x - 1 = 0$:

```
sage: t = var('t')           # define a variable t
sage: x = function('x',t)    # define x to be a function of that variable
sage: DE = diff(x, t) + x - 1
sage: desolve(DE, [x,t])
(c + e^t)*e^(-t)
```

This uses Sage's interface to Maxima [Max], and so its output may be a bit different from other Sage output. In this case, this says that the general solution to the differential equation is $x(t) = e^{-t}(e^t + c)$.

You can compute Laplace transforms also; the Laplace transform of $t^2 e^t - \sin(t)$ is computed as follows:

```
sage: s = var("s")
sage: t = var("t")
sage: f = t^2*exp(t) - sin(t)
sage: f.laplace(t,s)
-1/(s^2 + 1) + 2/(s - 1)^3
```

Here is a more involved example. The displacement from equilibrium (respectively) for a coupled spring attached to a wall on the left

```
|------\/\/\/\/\---|mass1|----\/\/\/\/\/----|mass2|
       spring1                spring2
```

is modeled by the system of 2nd order differential equations

$$m_1 x_1'' + (k_1 + k_2)x_1 - k_2 x_2 = 0$$
$$m_2 x_2'' + k_2(x_2 - x_1) = 0,$$

where m_i is the mass of object i, x_i is the displacement from equilibrium of mass i, and k_i is the spring constant for spring i.

Example: Use Sage to solve the above problem with $m_1 = 2$, $m_2 = 1$, $k_1 = 4$, $k_2 = 2$, $x_1(0) = 3$, $x_1'(0) = 0$, $x_2(0) = 3$, $x_2'(0) = 0$.

Solution: Take the Laplace transform of the first equation (with the notation $x = x_1$, $y = x_2$):

```
sage: de1 = maxima("2*diff(x(t),t, 2) + 6*x(t) - 2*y(t)")
sage: lde1 = de1.laplace("t","s");
```

The value of `lde1` is

$$-2x'(0) + 2s^2 \cdot X(s) - 2sx(0) - 2Y(s) + 6X(s) = 0$$

(where the Laplace transform of a lower case function like $x(t)$ is the upper case function $X(s)$). Take the Laplace transform of the second equation:

```
sage: de2 = maxima("diff(y(t),t, 2) + 2*y(t) - 2*x(t)")
sage: lde2 = de2.laplace("t","s");
```

The value of `lde2` is

$$-y'(0) + s^2 Y(s) + 2Y(s) - 2X(s) - sy(0) = 0.$$

Plug in the initial conditions for $x(0)$, $x'(0)$, $y(0)$, and $y'(0)$, and solve the resulting two equations:

```
sage: var('s X Y')
(s, X, Y)
sage: eqns = [(2*s^2+6)*X-2*Y == 6*s, -2*X +(s^2+2)*Y == 3*s]
sage: solve(eqns, X,Y)
[[X == 3*(s^3 + 3*s)/(s^4 + 5*s^2 + 4),
  Y == 3*(s^3 + 5*s)/(s^4 + 5*s^2 + 4)]]
```

Now take inverse Laplace transforms to get the answer:

```
sage: var('s t')
(s, t)
sage: inverse_laplace((3*s^3 + 9*s)/(s^4 + 5*s^2 + 4),s,t)
cos(2*t) + 2*cos(t)
sage: inverse_laplace((3*s^3 + 15*s)/(s^4 + 5*s^2 + 4),s,t)
-cos(2*t) + 4*cos(t)
```

Therefore, the solution is

$$x_1(t) = \cos(2t) + 2\cos(t), \quad x_2(t) = 4\cos(t) - \cos(2t).$$

This can be plotted parametrically using

```
sage: t = var('t')
sage: P = parametric_plot((cos(2*t) + 2*cos(t), 4*cos(t) - cos(2*t) ),\
...       (t, 0, 2*pi), rgbcolor=hue(0.9))
sage: show(P)
```

The individual components can be plotted using

```
sage: t = var('t')
sage: p1 = plot(cos(2*t) + 2*cos(t), (t,0, 2*pi), rgbcolor=hue(0.3))
sage: p2 = plot(4*cos(t) - cos(2*t), (t,0, 2*pi), rgbcolor=hue(0.6))
sage: show(p1 + p2)
```

For more on plotting, see *Plotting*. See section 5.5 of [NagleEtAl2004] for further information on differential equations.

2.4.4 Euler's Method for Systems of Differential Equations

In the next example, we will illustrate Euler's method for first and second order ODEs. We first recall the basic idea for first order equations. Given an initial value problem of the form

$$y' = f(x, y), \quad y(a) = c,$$

we want to find the approximate value of the solution at $x = b$ with $b > a$.

Recall from the definition of the derivative that

$$y'(x) \approx \frac{y(x+h) - y(x)}{h},$$

where $h > 0$ is given and small. This and the DE together give $f(x, y(x)) \approx \frac{y(x+h) - y(x)}{h}$. Now solve for $y(x+h)$:

$$y(x+h) \approx y(x) + h \cdot f(x, y(x)).$$

If we call $h \cdot f(x, y(x))$ the "correction term" (for lack of anything better), call $y(x)$ the "old value of y", and call $y(x+h)$ the "new value of y", then this approximation can be re-expressed as

$$y_{new} \approx y_{old} + h \cdot f(x, y_{old}).$$

If we break the interval from a to b into n steps, so that $h = \frac{b-a}{n}$, then we can record the information for this method in a table.

x	y	$h \cdot f(x, y)$
a	c	$h \cdot f(a, c)$
$a + h$	$c + h \cdot f(a, c)$	...
$a + 2h$	...	
...		
$b = a + nh$	???	...

The goal is to fill out all the blanks of the table, one row at a time, until we reach the ??? entry, which is the Euler's method approximation for $y(b)$.

The idea for systems of ODEs is similar.

Example: Numerically approximate $z(t)$ at $t = 1$ using 4 steps of Euler's method, where $z'' + tz' + z = 0$, $z(0) = 1$, $z'(0) = 0$.

We must reduce the 2nd order ODE down to a system of two first order DEs (using $x = z, y = z'$) and apply Euler's method:

```
sage: t,x,y = PolynomialRing(RealField(10),3,"txy").gens()
sage: f = y; g = -x - y*t
sage: eulers_method_2x2(f,g, 0, 1, 0, 1/4, 1)
     t          x         h*f(t,x,y)              y         h*g(t,x,y)
     0          1              0.00               0             -0.25
   1/4        1.0            -0.062           -0.25             -0.23
   1/2       0.94             -0.12           -0.48             -0.17
   3/4       0.82             -0.16           -0.66            -0.081
     1       0.65             -0.18           -0.74             0.022
```

Therefore, $z(1) \approx 0.65$.

We can also plot the points (x, y) to get an approximate picture of the curve. The function `eulers_method_2x2_plot` will do this; in order to use it, we need to define functions f and g which takes one argument with three coordinates: (t, x, y).

```
sage: f = lambda z: z[2]         # f(t,x,y) = y
sage: g = lambda z: -sin(z[1])   # g(t,x,y) = -sin(x)
sage: P = eulers_method_2x2_plot(f,g, 0.0, 0.75, 0.0, 0.1, 1.0)
```

At this point, P is storing two plots: `P[0]`, the plot of x vs. t, and `P[1]`, the plot of y vs. t. We can plot both of these as follows:

```
sage: show(P[0] + P[1])
```

(For more on plotting, see *Plotting*.)

2.4.5 Special functions

Several orthogonal polynomials and special functions are implemented, using both PARI [GAP] and Maxima [Max]. These are documented in the appropriate sections ("Orthogonal polynomials" and "Special functions", respectively) of the Sage reference manual.

```
sage: x = polygen(QQ, 'x')
sage: chebyshev_U(2,x)
4*x^2 - 1
sage: bessel_I(1,1).n(250)
0.56515910399248502720769602760986330732889962162109200948029448947925564096
sage: bessel_I(1,1).n()
0.565159103992485
sage: bessel_I(2,1.1).n()
0.167089499251049
```

At this point, Sage has only wrapped these functions for numerical use. For symbolic use, please use the Maxima interface directly, as in the following example:

```
sage: maxima.eval("f:bessel_y(v, w)")
'bessel_y(v,w)'
sage: maxima.eval("diff(f,w)")
'(bessel_y(v-1,w)-bessel_y(v+1,w))/2'
```

2.5 Plotting

Sage can produce two-dimensional and three-dimensional plots.

2.5.1 Two-dimensional Plots

In two dimensions, Sage can draw circles, lines, and polygons; plots of functions in rectangular coordinates; and also polar plots, contour plots and vector field plots. We present examples of some of these here. For more examples of plotting with Sage, see *Solving Differential Equations* and *Maxima*, and also the Sage Constructions documentation.

This command produces a yellow circle of radius 1, centered at the origin:

```
sage: circle((0,0), 1, rgbcolor=(1,1,0))
```

You can also produce a filled circle:

```
sage: circle((0,0), 1, rgbcolor=(1,1,0), fill=True)
```

You can also create a circle by assigning it to a variable; this does not plot it:

```
sage: c = circle((0,0), 1, rgbcolor=(1,1,0))
```

To plot it, use `c.show()` or `show(c)`, as follows:

```
sage: c.show()
```

Alternatively, evaluating `c.save('filename.png')` will save the plot to the given file.

Now, these 'circles' look more like ellipses because the axes are scaled differently. You can fix this:

```
sage: c.show(aspect_ratio=1)
```

The command `show(c, aspect_ratio=1)` accomplishes the same thing, or you can save the picture using `c.save('filename.png', aspect_ratio=1)`.

It's easy to plot basic functions:

```
sage: plot(cos, (-5,5))
```

Once you specify a variable name, you can create parametric plots also:

```
sage: x = var('x')
sage: parametric_plot((cos(x),sin(x)^3),(x,0,2*pi),rgbcolor=hue(0.6))
```

It's important to notice that the axes of the plots will only intersect if the origin is in the viewing range of the graph, and that with sufficiently large values scientific notation may be used:

```
sage: plot(x^2,(x,300,500))
```

You can combine several plots by adding them:

```
sage: x = var('x')
sage: p1 = parametric_plot((cos(x),sin(x)),(x,0,2*pi),rgbcolor=hue(0.2))
sage: p2 = parametric_plot((cos(x),sin(x)^2),(x,0,2*pi),rgbcolor=hue(0.4))
sage: p3 = parametric_plot((cos(x),sin(x)^3),(x,0,2*pi),rgbcolor=hue(0.6))
sage: show(p1+p2+p3, axes=false)
```

A good way to produce filled-in shapes is to produce a list of points (L in the example below) and then use the `polygon` command to plot the shape with boundary formed by those points. For example, here is a green deltoid:

```
sage: L = [[-1+cos(pi*i/100)*(1+cos(pi*i/100)),\
...        2*sin(pi*i/100)*(1-cos(pi*i/100))] for i in range(200)]
sage: p = polygon(L, rgbcolor=(1/8,3/4,1/2))
sage: p
```

Type `show(p, axes=false)` to see this without any axes.

You can add text to a plot:

```
sage: L = [[6*cos(pi*i/100)+5*cos((6/2)*pi*i/100),\
...        6*sin(pi*i/100)-5*sin((6/2)*pi*i/100)] for i in range(200)]
sage: p = polygon(L, rgbcolor=(1/8,1/4,1/2))
sage: t = text("hypotrochoid", (5,4), rgbcolor=(1,0,0))
sage: show(p+t)
```

Calculus teachers draw the following plot frequently on the board: not just one branch of arcsin but rather several of them: i.e., the plot of $y = \sin(x)$ for x between -2π and 2π, flipped about the 45 degree line. The following Sage commands construct this:

```
sage: v = [(sin(x),x) for x in srange(-2*float(pi),2*float(pi),0.1)]
sage: line(v)
```

2.5. Plotting

Since the tangent function has a larger range than sine, if you use the same trick to plot the inverse tangent, you should change the minimum and maximum coordinates for the *x*-axis:

```
sage: v = [(tan(x),x) for x in srange(-2*float(pi),2*float(pi),0.01)]
sage: show(line(v), xmin=-20, xmax=20)
```

Sage also computes polar plots, contour plots and vector field plots (for special types of functions). Here is an example of a contour plot:

```
sage: f = lambda x,y: cos(x*y)
sage: contour_plot(f, (-4, 4), (-4, 4))
```

2.5.2 Three-Dimensional Plots

Sage can also be used to create three-dimensional plots. In both the notebook and the REPL, these plots will be displayed by default using the open source package [Jmol], which supports interactively rotating and zooming the figure with the mouse.

Use `plot3d` to graph a function of the form $f(x, y) = z$:

```
sage: x, y = var('x,y')
sage: plot3d(x^2 + y^2, (x,-2,2), (y,-2,2))
```

Alternatively, you can use `parametric_plot3d` to graph a parametric surface where each of x, y, z is determined by a function of one or two variables (the parameters, typically u and v). The previous plot can be expressed parametrically as follows:

```
sage: u, v = var('u, v')
sage: f_x(u, v) = u
sage: f_y(u, v) = v
sage: f_z(u, v) = u^2 + v^2
sage: parametric_plot3d([f_x, f_y, f_z], (u, -2, 2), (v, -2, 2))
```

The third way to plot a 3D surface in Sage is `implicit_plot3d`, which graphs a contour of a function like $f(x, y, z) = 0$ (this defines a set of points). We graph a sphere using the classical formula:

```
sage: x, y, z = var('x, y, z')
sage: implicit_plot3d(x^2 + y^2 + z^2 - 4, (x,-2, 2), (y,-2, 2), (z,-2, 2))
```

Here are some more examples:

Yellow Whitney's umbrella:

```
sage: u, v = var('u,v')
sage: fx = u*v
sage: fy = u
sage: fz = v^2
sage: parametric_plot3d([fx, fy, fz], (u, -1, 1), (v, -1, 1),
...       frame=False, color="yellow")
```

Cross cap:

```
sage: u, v = var('u,v')
sage: fx = (1+cos(v))*cos(u)
sage: fy = (1+cos(v))*sin(u)
sage: fz = -tanh((2/3)*(u-pi))*sin(v)
sage: parametric_plot3d([fx, fy, fz], (u, 0, 2*pi), (v, 0, 2*pi),
....:     frame=False, color="red")
```

Twisted torus:

```
sage: u, v = var('u,v')
sage: fx = (3+sin(v)+cos(u))*cos(2*v)
sage: fy = (3+sin(v)+cos(u))*sin(2*v)
sage: fz = sin(u)+2*cos(v)
sage: parametric_plot3d([fx, fy, fz], (u, 0, 2*pi), (v, 0, 2*pi),
....:     frame=False, color="red")
```

Lemniscate:

```
sage: x, y, z = var('x,y,z')
sage: f(x, y, z) = 4*x^2 * (x^2 + y^2 + z^2 + z) + y^2 * (y^2 + z^2 - 1)
sage: implicit_plot3d(f, (x, -0.5, 0.5), (y, -1, 1), (z, -1, 1))
```

2.6 Some Common Issues with Functions

Some aspects of defining functions (e.g., for differentiation or plotting) can be confusing. In this section we try to address some of the relevant issues.

Here are several ways to define things which might deserve to be called "functions":

1. Define a Python function, as described in *Functions, Indentation, and Counting*. These functions can be plotted, but not differentiated or integrated.

```
sage: def f(z): return z^2
sage: type(f)
<type 'function'>
sage: f(3)
9
sage: plot(f, 0, 2)
```

In the last line, note the syntax. Using `plot(f(z), 0, 2)` instead will give an error, because z is a dummy variable in the definition of f and is not defined outside of that definition. Indeed, just `f(z)` returns an error. The following will work in this case, although in general there are issues and so it should probably be avoided (see item 4 below).

```
sage: var('z')   # define z to be a variable
z
sage: f(z)
z^2
sage: plot(f(z), 0, 2)
```

At this point, f(z) is a symbolic expression, the next item in our list.

2. Define a "callable symbolic expression". These can be plotted, differentiated, and integrated.

```
sage: g(x) = x^2
sage: g            # g sends x to x^2
x |--> x^2
sage: g(3)
9
sage: Dg = g.derivative(); Dg
x |--> 2*x
sage: Dg(3)
6
sage: type(g)
<type 'sage.symbolic.expression.Expression'>
sage: plot(g, 0, 2)
```

Note that while g is a callable symbolic expression, g(x) is a related, but different sort of object, which can also be plotted, differentated, etc., albeit with some issues: see item 5 below for an illustration.

```
sage: g(x)
x^2
sage: type(g(x))
<type 'sage.symbolic.expression.Expression'>
sage: g(x).derivative()
2*x
sage: plot(g(x), 0, 2)
```

3. Use a pre-defined Sage 'calculus function'. These can be plotted, and with a little help, differentiated, and integrated.

```
sage: type(sin)
<class 'sage.functions.trig.Function_sin'>
sage: plot(sin, 0, 2)
sage: type(sin(x))
<type 'sage.symbolic.expression.Expression'>
sage: plot(sin(x), 0, 2)
```

By itself, sin cannot be differentiated, at least not to produce cos.

```
sage: f = sin
sage: f.derivative()
Traceback (most recent call last):
...
AttributeError: ...
```

Using f = sin(x) instead of sin works, but it is probably even better to use f(x) = sin(x) to define a callable symbolic expression.

```
sage: S(x) = sin(x)
sage: S.derivative()
x |--> cos(x)
```

Here are some common problems, with explanations:

4. Accidental evaluation.

```
sage: def h(x):
...        if x<2:
...            return 0
...        else:
...            return x-2
```

The issue: `plot(h(x), 0, 4)` plots the line $y = x - 2$, not the multi-line function defined by h. The reason? In the command `plot(h(x), 0, 4)`, first `h(x)` is evaluated: this means plugging x into the function h, which means that x<2 is evaluated.

```
sage: type(x<2)
<type 'sage.symbolic.expression.Expression'>
```

When a symbolic equation is evaluated, as in the definition of h, if it is not obviously true, then it returns False. Thus `h(x)` evaluates to `x-2`, and this is the function that gets plotted.

The solution: don't use `plot(h(x), 0, 4)`; instead, use

```
sage: plot(h, 0, 4)
```

5. Accidentally producing a constant instead of a function.

```
sage: f = x
sage: g = f.derivative()
sage: g
1
```

The problem: `g(3)`, for example, returns an error, saying "ValueError: the number of arguments must be less than or equal to 0."

```
sage: type(f)
<type 'sage.symbolic.expression.Expression'>
sage: type(g)
<type 'sage.symbolic.expression.Expression'>
```

g is not a function, it's a constant, so it has no variables associated to it, and you can't plug anything into it.

The solution: there are several options.

- Define f initially to be a symbolic expression.

```
sage: f(x) = x          # instead of 'f = x'
sage: g = f.derivative()
sage: g
x |--> 1
sage: g(3)
1
sage: type(g)
<type 'sage.symbolic.expression.Expression'>
```

- Or with f as defined originally, define g to be a symbolic expression.

```
sage: f = x
sage: g(x) = f.derivative()   # instead of 'g = f.derivative()'
```

2.6. Some Common Issues with Functions

```
sage: g
x |--> 1
sage: g(3)
1
sage: type(g)
<type 'sage.symbolic.expression.Expression'>
```

- Or with `f` and `g` as defined originally, specify the variable for which you are substituting.

```
sage: f = x
sage: g = f.derivative()
sage: g
1
sage: g(x=3)     # instead of 'g(3)'
1
```

Finally, here's one more way to tell the difference between the derivatives of `f = x` and `f(x) = x`

```
sage: f(x) = x
sage: g = f.derivative()
sage: g.variables()   # the variables present in g
()
sage: g.arguments()   # the arguments which can be plugged into g
(x,)
sage: f = x
sage: h = f.derivative()
sage: h.variables()
()
sage: h.arguments()
()
```

As this example has been trying to illustrate, `h` accepts no arguments, and this is why `h(3)` returns an error.

2.7 Basic Rings

When defining matrices, vectors, or polynomials, it is sometimes useful and sometimes necessary to specify the "ring" over which it is defined. A *ring* is a mathematical construction in which there are well-behaved notions of addition and multiplication; if you've never heard of them before, you probably just need to know about these four commonly used rings:

- the integers $\{..., -1, 0, 1, 2, ...\}$, called `ZZ` in Sage.
- the rational numbers – i.e., fractions, or ratios, of integers – called `QQ` in Sage.
- the real numbers, called `RR` in Sage.
- the complex numbers, called `CC` in Sage.

You may need to know about these distinctions because the same polynomial, for example, can be treated differently depending on the ring over which it is defined. For instance, the polynomial $x^2 - 2$ has two roots, $\pm\sqrt{2}$. Those roots are not rational, so if you are working with polynomials with rational coefficients, the polynomial won't factor. With real coefficients, it will. Therefore you may want to specify the ring to insure

that you are getting the information you expect. The following two commands defines the sets of polynomials
with rational coefficients and real coefficients, respectively. The sets are named "ratpoly" and "realpoly", but
these aren't important here; however, note that the strings ".<t>" and ".<z>" name the *variables* used in the
two cases.

```
sage: ratpoly.<t> = PolynomialRing(QQ)
sage: realpoly.<z> = PolynomialRing(RR)
```

Now we illustrate the point about factoring $x^2 - 2$:

```
sage: factor(t^2-2)
t^2 - 2
sage: factor(z^2-2)
(z - 1.41421356237310) * (z + 1.41421356237310)
```

Similar comments apply to matrices: the row-reduced form of a matrix can depend on the ring over which it is
defined, as can its eigenvalues and eigenvectors. For more about constructing polynomials, see *Polynomials*,
and for more about matrices, see *Linear Algebra*.

The symbol I represents the square root of -1; i is a synonym for I. Of course, this is not a rational number:

```
sage: i        # square root of -1
I
sage: i in QQ
False
```

Note: The above code may not work as expected if the variable i has been assigned a different value, for
example, if it was used as a loop variable. If this is the case, type

```
sage: reset('i')
```

to get the original complex value of i.

There is one subtlety in defining complex numbers: as mentioned above, the symbol i represents a square
root of -1, but it is a *formal* or *symbolic* square root of -1. Calling CC(i) or CC.0 returns the *complex*
square root of -1. Arithmetic involving different kinds of numbers is possible by so-called coercion, see
Parents, Conversion and Coercion.

```
sage: i = CC(i)       # floating point complex number
sage: i == CC.0
True
sage: a, b = 4/3, 2/3
sage: z = a + b*i
sage: z
1.33333333333333 + 0.666666666666667*I
sage: z.imag()        # imaginary part
0.666666666666667
sage: z.real() == a   # automatic coercion before comparison
True
sage: a + b
2
sage: 2*b == a
True
sage: parent(2/3)
```

2.7. Basic Rings

```
Rational Field
sage: parent(4/2)
Rational Field
sage: 2/3 + 0.1        # automatic coercion before addition
0.766666666666667
sage: 0.1 + 2/3        # coercion rules are symmetric in SAGE
0.766666666666667
```

Here are more examples of basic rings in Sage. As noted above, the ring of rational numbers may be referred to using QQ, or also `RationalField()` (a *field* is a ring in which the multiplication is commutative and in which every nonzero element has a reciprocal in that ring, so the rationals form a field, but the integers don't):

```
sage: RationalField()
Rational Field
sage: QQ
Rational Field
sage: 1/2 in QQ
True
```

The decimal number 1.2 is considered to be in QQ: decimal numbers which happen to also be rational can be "coerced" into the rational numbers (see *Parents, Conversion and Coercion*). The numbers π and $\sqrt{2}$ are not rational, though:

```
sage: 1.2 in QQ
True
sage: pi in QQ
False
sage: pi in RR
True
sage: sqrt(2) in QQ
False
sage: sqrt(2) in CC
True
```

For use in higher mathematics, Sage also knows about other rings, such as finite fields, *p*-adic integers, the ring of algebraic numbers, polynomial rings, and matrix rings. Here are constructions of some of these:

```
sage: GF(3)
Finite Field of size 3
sage: GF(27, 'a')   # need to name the generator if not a prime field
Finite Field in a of size 3^3
sage: Zp(5)
5-adic Ring with capped relative precision 20
sage: sqrt(3) in QQbar # algebraic closure of QQ
True
```

2.8 Linear Algebra

Sage provides standard constructions from linear algebra, e.g., the characteristic polynomial, echelon form, trace, decomposition, etc., of a matrix.

Creation of matrices and matrix multiplication is easy and natural:

```
sage: A = Matrix([[1,2,3],[3,2,1],[1,1,1]])
sage: w = vector([1,1,-4])
sage: w*A
(0, 0, 0)
sage: A*w
(-9, 1, -2)
sage: kernel(A)
Free module of degree 3 and rank 1 over Integer Ring
Echelon basis matrix:
[ 1  1 -4]
```

Note that in Sage, the kernel of a matrix A is the "left kernel", i.e. the space of vectors w such that $wA = 0$.

Solving matrix equations is easy, using the method `solve_right`. Evaluating `A.solve_right(Y)` returns a matrix (or vector) X so that $AX = Y$:

```
sage: Y = vector([0, -4, -1])
sage: X = A.solve_right(Y)
sage: X
(-2, 1, 0)
sage: A * X    # checking our answer...
(0, -4, -1)
```

A backslash \ can be used in the place of `solve_right`; use `A \ Y` instead of `A.solve_right(Y)`.

```
sage: A \ Y
(-2, 1, 0)
```

If there is no solution, Sage returns an error:

```
sage: A.solve_right(w)
Traceback (most recent call last):
...
ValueError: matrix equation has no solutions
```

Similarly, use `A.solve_left(Y)` to solve for X in $XA = Y$.

Sage can also compute eigenvalues and eigenvectors:

```
sage: A = matrix([[0, 4], [-1, 0]])
sage: A.eigenvalues ()
[-2*I, 2*I]
sage: B = matrix([[1, 3], [3, 1]])
sage: B.eigenvectors_left()
[(4, [
(1, 1)
], 1), (-2, [
```

```
(1, -1)
], 1)]
```

(The syntax for the output of `eigenvectors_left` is a list of triples: (eigenvalue, eigenvector, multiplicity).) Eigenvalues and eigenvectors over QQ or RR can also be computed using Maxima (see *Maxima* below).

As noted in *Basic Rings*, the ring over which a matrix is defined affects some of its properties. In the following, the first argument to the `matrix` command tells Sage to view the matrix as a matrix of integers (the ZZ case), a matrix of rational numbers (QQ), or a matrix of reals (RR):

```
sage: AZ = matrix(ZZ, [[2,0], [0,1]])
sage: AQ = matrix(QQ, [[2,0], [0,1]])
sage: AR = matrix(RR, [[2,0], [0,1]])
sage: AZ.echelon_form()
[2 0]
[0 1]
sage: AQ.echelon_form()
[1 0]
[0 1]
sage: AR.echelon_form()
[ 1.00000000000000 0.000000000000000]
[0.000000000000000  1.00000000000000]
```

For computing eigenvalues and eigenvectors of matrices over floating point real or complex numbers, the matrix should be defined over RDF (Real Double Field) or CDF (Complex Double Field), respectively. If no ring is specified and floating point real or complex numbers are used then by default the matrix is defined over the RR or CC fields, respectively, which do not support these computations for all the cases:

```
sage: ARDF = matrix(RDF, [[1.2, 2], [2, 3]])
sage: ARDF.eigenvalues()
[-0.0931712199461, 4.29317121995]
sage: ACDF = matrix(CDF, [[1.2, I], [2, 3]])
sage: ACDF.eigenvectors_right()
[(0.881845698329 - 0.820914065343*I,
 [(0.750560818381, -0.616145932705 + 0.238794153033*I)], 1),
 (3.31815430167 + 0.820914065343*I,
 [(0.145594698293 + 0.37566908585*I, 0.915245825866)], 1)]
```

2.8.1 Matrix spaces

We create the space $\text{Mat}_{3\times 3}(\mathbf{Q})$ of 3×3 matrices with rational entries:

```
sage: M = MatrixSpace(QQ,3)
sage: M
Full MatrixSpace of 3 by 3 dense matrices over Rational Field
```

(To specify the space of 3 by 4 matrices, you would use `MatrixSpace(QQ,3,4)`. If the number of columns is omitted, it defaults to the number of rows, so `MatrixSpace(QQ,3)` is a synonym for `MatrixSpace(QQ,3,3)`.) The space of matrices has a basis which Sage stores as a list:

```
sage: B = M.basis()
sage: len(B)
9
sage: B[1]
[0 1 0]
[0 0 0]
[0 0 0]
```

We create a matrix as an element of M.

```
sage: A = M(range(9)); A
[0 1 2]
[3 4 5]
[6 7 8]
```

Next we compute its reduced row echelon form and kernel.

```
sage: A.echelon_form()
[ 1  0 -1]
[ 0  1  2]
[ 0  0  0]
sage: A.kernel()
Vector space of degree 3 and dimension 1 over Rational Field
Basis matrix:
[ 1 -2  1]
```

Next we illustrate computation of matrices defined over finite fields:

```
sage: M = MatrixSpace(GF(2),4,8)
sage: A = M([1,1,0,0, 1,1,1,1, 0,1,0,0, 1,0,1,1,
...          0,0,1,0, 1,1,0,1, 0,0,1,1, 1,1,1,0])
sage: A
[1 1 0 0 1 1 1 1]
[0 1 0 0 1 0 1 1]
[0 0 1 0 1 1 0 1]
[0 0 1 1 1 1 1 0]
sage: rows = A.rows()
sage: A.columns()
[(1, 0, 0, 0), (1, 1, 0, 0), (0, 0, 1, 1), (0, 0, 0, 1),
 (1, 1, 1, 1), (1, 0, 1, 1), (1, 1, 0, 1), (1, 1, 1, 0)]
sage: rows
[(1, 1, 0, 0, 1, 1, 1, 1), (0, 1, 0, 0, 1, 0, 1, 1),
 (0, 0, 1, 0, 1, 1, 0, 1), (0, 0, 1, 1, 1, 1, 1, 0)]
```

We make the subspace over $\mathbf{F}_2$ spanned by the above rows.

```
sage: V = VectorSpace(GF(2),8)
sage: S = V.subspace(rows)
sage: S
Vector space of degree 8 and dimension 4 over Finite Field of size 2
Basis matrix:
[1 0 0 0 0 1 0 0]
[0 1 0 0 1 0 1 1]
```

```
[0 0 1 0 1 1 0 1]
[0 0 0 1 0 0 1 1]
sage: A.echelon_form()
[1 0 0 0 0 1 0 0]
[0 1 0 0 1 0 1 1]
[0 0 1 0 1 1 0 1]
[0 0 0 1 0 0 1 1]
```

The basis of S used by Sage is obtained from the non-zero rows of the reduced row echelon form of the matrix of generators of S.

2.8.2 Sparse Linear Algebra

Sage has support for sparse linear algebra over PIDs.

```
sage: M = MatrixSpace(QQ, 100, sparse=True)
sage: A = M.random_element(density = 0.05)
sage: E = A.echelon_form()
```

The multi-modular algorithm in Sage is good for square matrices (but not so good for non-square matrices):

```
sage: M = MatrixSpace(QQ, 50, 100, sparse=True)
sage: A = M.random_element(density = 0.05)
sage: E = A.echelon_form()
sage: M = MatrixSpace(GF(2), 20, 40, sparse=True)
sage: A = M.random_element()
sage: E = A.echelon_form()
```

Note that Python is case sensitive:

```
sage: M = MatrixSpace(QQ, 10,10, Sparse=True)
Traceback (most recent call last):
...
TypeError: __classcall__() got an unexpected keyword argument 'Sparse'
```

2.9 Polynomials

In this section we illustrate how to create and use polynomials in Sage.

2.9.1 Univariate Polynomials

There are three ways to create polynomial rings.

```
sage: R = PolynomialRing(QQ, 't')
sage: R
Univariate Polynomial Ring in t over Rational Field
```

This creates a polynomial ring and tells Sage to use (the string) 't' as the indeterminate when printing to the screen. However, this does not define the symbol t for use in Sage, so you cannot use it to enter a polynomial (such as $t^2 + 1$) belonging to R.

An alternate way is

```
sage: S = QQ['t']
sage: S == R
True
```

This has the same issue regarding t.

A third very convenient way is

```
sage: R.<t> = PolynomialRing(QQ)
```

or

```
sage: R.<t> = QQ['t']
```

or even

```
sage: R.<t> = QQ[]
```

This has the additional side effect that it defines the variable t to be the indeterminate of the polynomial ring, so you can easily construct elements of R, as follows. (Note that the third way is very similar to the constructor notation in Magma, and just as in Magma it can be used for a wide range of objects.)

```
sage: poly = (t+1) * (t+2); poly
t^2 + 3*t + 2
sage: poly in R
True
```

Whatever method you use to define a polynomial ring, you can recover the indeterminate as the 0th generator:

```
sage: R = PolynomialRing(QQ, 't')
sage: t = R.0
sage: t in R
True
```

Note that a similar construction works with the complex numbers: the complex numbers can be viewed as being generated over the real numbers by the symbol i; thus we have the following:

```
sage: CC
Complex Field with 53 bits of precision
sage: CC.0    # 0th generator of CC
1.00000000000000*I
```

For polynomial rings, you can obtain both the ring and its generator, or just the generator, during ring creation as follows:

```
sage: R, t = QQ['t'].objgen()
sage: t    = QQ['t'].gen()
sage: R, t = objgen(QQ['t'])
sage: t    = gen(QQ['t'])
```

Finally we do some arithmetic in $\mathbf{Q}[t]$.

```
sage: R, t = QQ['t'].objgen()
sage: f = 2*t^7 + 3*t^2 - 15/19
sage: f^2
4*t^14 + 12*t^9 - 60/19*t^7 + 9*t^4 - 90/19*t^2 + 225/361
sage: cyclo = R.cyclotomic_polynomial(7); cyclo
t^6 + t^5 + t^4 + t^3 + t^2 + t + 1
sage: g = 7 * cyclo * t^5 * (t^5 + 10*t + 2)
sage: g
7*t^16 + 7*t^15 + 7*t^14 + 7*t^13 + 77*t^12 + 91*t^11 + 91*t^10 + 84*t^9
    + 84*t^8 + 84*t^7 + 84*t^6 + 14*t^5
sage: F = factor(g); F
(7) * t^5 * (t^5 + 10*t + 2) * (t^6 + t^5 + t^4 + t^3 + t^2 + t + 1)
sage: F.unit()
7
sage: list(F)
[(t, 5), (t^5 + 10*t + 2, 1), (t^6 + t^5 + t^4 + t^3 + t^2 + t + 1, 1)]
```

Notice that the factorization correctly takes into account and records the unit part.

If you were to use, e.g., the R.cyclotomic_polynomial function a lot for some research project, in addition to citing Sage you should make an attempt to find out what component of Sage is being used to actually compute the cyclotomic polynomial and cite that as well. In this case, if you type R.cyclotomic_polynomial?? to see the source code, you'll quickly see a line f = pari.polcyclo(n) which means that PARI is being used for computation of the cyclotomic polynomial. Cite PARI in your work as well.

Dividing two polynomials constructs an element of the fraction field (which Sage creates automatically).

```
sage: x = QQ['x'].0
sage: f = x^3 + 1; g = x^2 - 17
sage: h = f/g;  h
(x^3 + 1)/(x^2 - 17)
sage: h.parent()
Fraction Field of Univariate Polynomial Ring in x over Rational Field
```

Using Laurent series, one can compute series expansions in the fraction field of QQ[x]:

```
sage: R.<x> = LaurentSeriesRing(QQ); R
Laurent Series Ring in x over Rational Field
sage: 1/(1-x) + O(x^10)
1 + x + x^2 + x^3 + x^4 + x^5 + x^6 + x^7 + x^8 + x^9 + O(x^10)
```

If we name the variable differently, we obtain a different univariate polynomial ring.

```
sage: R.<x> = PolynomialRing(QQ)
sage: S.<y> = PolynomialRing(QQ)
sage: x == y
False
sage: R == S
False
sage: R(y)
x
```

```
sage: R(y^2 - 17)
x^2 - 17
```

The ring is determined by the variable. Note that making another ring with variable called x does not return a different ring.

```
sage: R = PolynomialRing(QQ, "x")
sage: T = PolynomialRing(QQ, "x")
sage: R == T
True
sage: R is T
True
sage: R.0 == T.0
True
```

Sage also has support for power series and Laurent series rings over any base ring. In the following example, we create an element of $\mathbf{F}_7[[T]]$ and divide to create an element of $\mathbf{F}_7((T))$.

```
sage: R.<T> = PowerSeriesRing(GF(7)); R
Power Series Ring in T over Finite Field of size 7
sage: f = T + 3*T^2 + T^3 + O(T^4)
sage: f^3
T^3 + 2*T^4 + 2*T^5 + O(T^6)
sage: 1/f
T^-1 + 4 + T + O(T^2)
sage: parent(1/f)
Laurent Series Ring in T over Finite Field of size 7
```

You can also create power series rings using a double-brackets shorthand:

```
sage: GF(7)[['T']]
Power Series Ring in T over Finite Field of size 7
```

2.9.2 Multivariate Polynomials

To work with polynomials of several variables, we declare the polynomial ring and variables first.

```
sage: R = PolynomialRing(GF(5),3,"z") # here, 3 = number of variables
sage: R
Multivariate Polynomial Ring in z0, z1, z2 over Finite Field of size 5
```

Just as for defining univariate polynomial rings, there are alternative ways:

```
sage: GF(5)['z0, z1, z2']
Multivariate Polynomial Ring in z0, z1, z2 over Finite Field of size 5
sage: R.<z0,z1,z2> = GF(5)[]; R
Multivariate Polynomial Ring in z0, z1, z2 over Finite Field of size 5
```

Also, if you want the variable names to be single letters then you can use the following shorthand:

```
sage: PolynomialRing(GF(5), 3, 'xyz')
Multivariate Polynomial Ring in x, y, z over Finite Field of size 5
```

2.9. Polynomials

Next let's do some arithmetic.

```
sage: z = GF(5)['z0, z1, z2'].gens()
sage: z
(z0, z1, z2)
sage: (z[0]+z[1]+z[2])^2
z0^2 + 2*z0*z1 + z1^2 + 2*z0*z2 + 2*z1*z2 + z2^2
```

You can also use more mathematical notation to construct a polynomial ring.

```
sage: R = GF(5)['x,y,z']
sage: x,y,z = R.gens()
sage: QQ['x']
Univariate Polynomial Ring in x over Rational Field
sage: QQ['x,y'].gens()
(x, y)
sage: QQ['x'].objgens()
(Univariate Polynomial Ring in x over Rational Field, (x,))
```

Multivariate polynomials are implemented in Sage using Python dictionaries and the "distributive representation" of a polynomial. Sage makes some use of Singular [Si], e.g., for computation of gcd's and Gröbner basis of ideals.

```
sage: R, (x, y) = PolynomialRing(RationalField(), 2, 'xy').objgens()
sage: f = (x^3 + 2*y^2*x)^2
sage: g = x^2*y^2
sage: f.gcd(g)
x^2
```

Next we create the ideal (f, g) generated by f and g, by simply multiplying (f, g) by R (we could also write ideal([f,g]) or ideal(f,g)).

```
sage: I = (f, g)*R; I
Ideal (x^6 + 4*x^4*y^2 + 4*x^2*y^4, x^2*y^2) of Multivariate Polynomial
Ring in x, y over Rational Field
sage: B = I.groebner_basis(); B
[x^6, x^2*y^2]
sage: x^2 in I
False
```

Incidentally, the Gröbner basis above is not a list but an immutable sequence. This means that it has a universe, parent, and cannot be changed (which is good because changing the basis would break other routines that use the Gröbner basis).

```
sage: B.parent()
Category of sequences in Multivariate Polynomial Ring in x, y over Rational
Field
sage: B.universe()
Multivariate Polynomial Ring in x, y over Rational Field
sage: B[1] = x
Traceback (most recent call last):
...
ValueError: object is immutable; please change a copy instead.
```

Some (read: not as much as we would like) commutative algebra is available in Sage, implemented via Singular. For example, we can compute the primary decomposition and associated primes of I:

```
sage: I.primary_decomposition()
[Ideal (x^2) of Multivariate Polynomial Ring in x, y over Rational Field,
 Ideal (y^2, x^6) of Multivariate Polynomial Ring in x, y over Rational Field]
sage: I.associated_primes()
[Ideal (x) of Multivariate Polynomial Ring in x, y over Rational Field,
 Ideal (y, x) of Multivariate Polynomial Ring in x, y over Rational Field]
```

2.10 Parents, Conversion and Coercion

This section may seem more technical than the previous, but we believe that it is important to understand the meaning of parents and coercion in order to use rings and other algebraic structures in Sage effectively and efficiently.

Note that we try to explain notions, but we do not show here how to implement them. An implementation-oriented tutorial is available as a Sage thematic tutorial.

2.10.1 Elements

If one wants to implement a ring in Python, a first approximation is to create a class for the elements X of that ring and provide it with the required double underscore methods such as __add__, __sub__, __mul__, of course making sure that the ring axioms hold.

As Python is a strongly typed (yet dynamically typed) language, one might, at least at first, expect that one implements one Python class for each ring. After all, Python contains one type <int> for the integers, one type <float> for the reals, and so on. But that approach must soon fail: There are infinitely many rings, and one can not implement infinitely many classes.

Instead, one may create a hierarchy of classes designed to implement elements of ubiquitous algebraic structures, such as groups, rings, skew fields, commutative rings, fields, algebras, and so on.

But that means that elements of fairly different rings can have the same type.

```
sage: P.<x,y> = GF(3)[]
sage: Q.<a,b> = GF(4,'z')[]
sage: type(x)==type(a)
True
```

On the other hand, one could also have different Python classes providing different implementations of the same mathematical structure (e.g., dense matrices versus sparse matrices)

```
sage: P.<a> = PolynomialRing(ZZ)
sage: Q.<b> = PolynomialRing(ZZ, sparse=True)
sage: R.<c> = PolynomialRing(ZZ, implementation='NTL')
sage: type(a); type(b); type(c)
<type 'sage.[...].polynomial_integer_dense_flint.Polynomial_integer_dense_flint'>
<class 'sage.[...].polynomial_element_generic.Polynomial_generic_sparse'>
<type 'sage.[...].polynomial_integer_dense_ntl.Polynomial_integer_dense_ntl'>
```

That poses two problems: On the one hand, if one has elements that are two instances of the same class, then one may expect that their __add__ method will allow to add them; but one does not want that, if the elements belong to very different rings. On the other hand, if one has elements belonging to different implementations of the same ring, then one wants to add them, but that is not straight forward if they belong to different Python classes.

The solution to these problems is called "coercion" and will be explained below.

However, it is essential that each element knows what it is element of. That is available by the method `parent()`:

```
sage: a.parent(); b.parent(); c.parent()
Univariate Polynomial Ring in a over Integer Ring
Sparse Univariate Polynomial Ring in b over Integer Ring
Univariate Polynomial Ring in c over Integer Ring (using NTL)
```

2.10.2 Parents and categories

Similar to the hierarchy of Python classes addressed to elements of algebraic structures, Sage also provides classes for the algebraic structures that contain these elements. Structures containing elements are called "parent structures" in Sage, and there is a base class for them. Roughly parallel to the hierarchy of mathematical notions, one has a hierarchy of classes, namely for sets, rings, fields, and so on:

```
sage: isinstance(QQ,Field)
True
sage: isinstance(QQ, Ring)
True
sage: isinstance(ZZ,Field)
False
sage: isinstance(ZZ, Ring)
True
```

In algebra, objects sharing the same kind of algebraic structures are collected in so-called "categories". So, there is a rough analogy between the class hierarchy in Sage and the hierarchy of categories. However, this analogy of Python classes and categories shouldn't be stressed too much. After all, mathematical categories are implemented in Sage as well:

```
sage: Rings()
Category of rings
sage: ZZ.category()
Category of euclidean domains
sage: ZZ.category().is_subcategory(Rings())
True
sage: ZZ in Rings()
True
sage: ZZ in Fields()
False
sage: QQ in Fields()
True
```

While Sage's class hierarchy is centered at implementation details, Sage's category framework is more centered on mathematical structure. It is possible to implement generic methods and tests independent of a specific implementation in the categories.

Parent structures in Sage are supposed to be unique Python objects. For example, once a polynomial ring over a certain base ring and with a certain list of generators is created, the result is cached:

```
sage: RR['x','y'] is RR['x','y']
True
```

2.10.3 Types versus parents

The type `RingElement` should not be confused with the mathematical notion of a ring element; for practical reasons, sometimes an object is an instance of `RingElement` although it does not belong to a ring:

```
sage: M = Matrix(ZZ,2,3); M
[0 0 0]
[0 0 0]
sage: isinstance(M, RingElement)
True
```

While *parents* are unique, equal *elements* of a parent in Sage are not necessarily identical. This is in contrast to the behaviour of Python for some (albeit not all) integers:

```
sage: int(1) is int(1)    # Python int
True
sage: int(-15) is int(-15)
False
sage: 1 is 1              # Sage Integer
False
```

It is important to observe that elements of different rings are in general not distinguished by their type, but by their parent:

```
sage: a = GF(2)(1)
sage: b = GF(5)(1)
sage: type(a) is type(b)
True
sage: parent(a)
Finite Field of size 2
sage: parent(b)
Finite Field of size 5
```

Hence, from an algebraic point of view, **the parent of an element is more important than its type.**

2.10.4 Conversion versus Coercion

In some cases it is possible to convert an element of one parent structure into an element of a different parent structure. Such conversion can either be explicit or implicit (this is called *coercion*).

The reader may know the notions *type conversion* and *type coercion* from, e.g., the C programming language. There are notions of *conversion* and *coercion* in Sage as well. But the notions in Sage are centered on *parents*, not on types. So, please don't confuse type conversion in C with conversion in Sage!

We give here a rather brief account. For a detailed description and for information on the implementation, we refer to the section on coercion in the reference manual and to the thematic tutorial.

There are two extremal positions concerning the possibility of doing arithmetic with elements of *different* rings:

- Different rings are different worlds, and it makes no sense whatsoever to add or multiply elements of different rings; even `1 + 1/2` makes no sense, since the first summand is an integer and the second a rational.

Or

- If an element `r1` of one ring `R1` can somehow be interpreted in another ring `R2`, then all arithmetic operations involving `r1` and any element of `R2` are allowed. The multiplicative unit exists in all fields and many rings, and they should all be equal.

Sage favours a compromise. If `P1` and `P2` are parent structures and `p1` is an element of `P1`, then the user may explicitly ask for an interpretation of `p1` in `P2`. This may not be meaningful in all cases or not be defined for all elements of `P1`, and it is up to the user to ensure that it makes sense. We refer to this as **conversion**:

```
sage: a = GF(2)(1)
sage: b = GF(5)(1)
sage: GF(5)(a) == b
True
sage: GF(2)(b) == a
True
```

However, an *implicit* (or automatic) conversion will only happen if this can be done *thoroughly* and *consistently*. Mathematical rigour is essential at that point.

Such an implicit conversion is called **coercion**. If coercion is defined, then it must coincide with conversion. Two conditions must be satisfied for a coercion to be defined:

1. A coercion from `P1` to `P2` must be given by a structure preserving map (e.g., a ring homomorphism). It does not suffice that *some* elements of `P1` can be mapped to `P2`, and the map must respect the algebraic structure of `P1`.

2. The choice of these coercion maps must be consistent: If `P3` is a third parent structure, then the composition of the chosen coercion from `P1` to `P2` with the coercion from `P2` to `P3` must coincide with the chosen coercion from `P1` to `P3`. In particular, if there is a coercion from `P1` to `P2` and `P2` to `P1`, the composition must be the identity map of `P1`.

So, although it is possible to convert each element of `GF(2)` into `GF(5)`, there is no coercion, since there is no ring homomorphism between `GF(2)` and `GF(5)`.

The second aspect - consistency - is a bit more difficult to explain. We illustrate it with multivariate polynomial rings. In applications, it certainly makes most sense to have name preserving coercions. So, we have:

```
sage: R1.<x,y> = ZZ[]
sage: R2 = ZZ['y','x']
sage: R2.has_coerce_map_from(R1)
True
sage: R2(x)
x
```

```
sage: R2(y)
y
```

If there is no name preserving ring homomorphism, coercion is not defined. However, conversion may still be possible, namely by mapping ring generators according to their position in the list of generators:

```
sage: R3 = ZZ['z','x']
sage: R3.has_coerce_map_from(R1)
False
sage: R3(x)
z
sage: R3(y)
x
```

But such position preserving conversions do not qualify as coercion: By composing a name preserving map from `ZZ['x','y']` to `ZZ['y','x']` with a position preserving map from `ZZ['y','x']` to `ZZ['a','b']`, a map would result that is neither name preserving nor position preserving, in violation to consistency.

If there is a coercion, it will be used to compare elements of different rings or to do arithmetic. This is often convenient, but the user should be aware that extending the ==-relation across the borders of different parents may easily result in overdoing it. For example, while == is supposed to be an equivalence relation on the elements of *one* ring, this is not necessarily the case if *different* rings are involved. For example, 1 in ZZ and in a finite field are considered equal, since there is a canonical coercion from the integers to any finite field. However, in general there is no coercion between two different finite fields. Therefore we have

```
sage: GF(5)(1) == 1
True
sage: 1 == GF(2)(1)
True
sage: GF(5)(1) == GF(2)(1)
False
sage: GF(5)(1) != GF(2)(1)
True
```

Similarly, we have

```
sage: R3(R1.1) == R3.1
True
sage: R1.1 == R3.1
False
sage: R1.1 != R3.1
True
```

Another consequence of the consistency condition is that coercions can only go from exact rings (e.g., the rationals QQ) to inexact rings (e.g., real numbers with a fixed precision RR), but not the other way around. The reason is that the composition of the coercion from QQ to RR with a conversion from RR to QQ is supposed to be the identity on QQ. But this is impossible, since some distinct rational numbers may very well be treated equal in RR, as in the following example:

```
sage: RR(1/10^200+1/10^100) == RR(1/10^100)
True
```

```
sage: 1/10^200+1/10^100 == 1/10^100
False
```

When comparing elements of two parents `P1` and `P2`, it is possible that there is no coercion between the two rings, but there is a canonical choice of a parent `P3` so that both `P1` and `P2` coerce into `P3`. In this case, coercion will take place as well. A typical use case is the sum of a rational number and a polynomial with integer coefficients, yielding a polynomial with rational coefficients:

```
sage: P1.<x> = ZZ[]
sage: p = 2*x+3
sage: q = 1/2
sage: parent(p)
Univariate Polynomial Ring in x over Integer Ring
sage: parent(p+q)
Univariate Polynomial Ring in x over Rational Field
```

Note that in principle the result would also make sense in the fraction field of `ZZ['x']`. However, Sage tries to choose a *canonical* common parent that seems to be most natural (`QQ['x']` in our example). If several potential common parents seem equally natural, Sage will *not* pick one of them at random, in order to have a reliable result. The mechanisms which that choice is based upon is explained in the thematic tutorial.

No coercion into a common parent will take place in the following example:

```
sage: R.<x> = QQ[]
sage: S.<y> = QQ[]
sage: x+y
Traceback (most recent call last):
...
TypeError: unsupported operand parent(s) for '+':
'Univar. Poly. Ring in x over Rat. Field' and 'Univar. Poly. Ring in y over Rat. Field'
```

The reason is that Sage would not choose one of the potential candidates `QQ['x']['y']`, `QQ['y']['x']`, `QQ['x','y']` or `QQ['y','x']`, because all of these four pairwise different structures seem natural common parents, and there is no apparent canonical choice.

2.11 Finite Groups, Abelian Groups

Sage has some support for computing with permutation groups, finite classical groups (such as $SU(n,q)$), finite matrix groups (with your own generators), and abelian groups (even infinite ones). Much of this is implemented using the interface to GAP.

For example, to create a permutation group, give a list of generators, as in the following example.

```
sage: G = PermutationGroup(['(1,2,3)(4,5)', '(3,4)'])
sage: G
Permutation Group with generators [(3,4), (1,2,3)(4,5)]
sage: G.order()
120
sage: G.is_abelian()
```

```
False
sage: G.derived_series()                # random-ish output
[Permutation Group with generators [(1,2,3)(4,5), (3,4)],
 Permutation Group with generators [(1,5)(3,4), (1,5)(2,4), (1,3,5)]]
sage: G.center()
Subgroup of (Permutation Group with generators [(3,4), (1,2,3)(4,5)]) generated by [()]
sage: G.random_element()                # random output
(1,5,3)(2,4)
sage: print latex(G)
\langle (3,4), (1,2,3)(4,5) \rangle
```

You can also obtain the character table (in LaTeX format) in Sage:

```
sage: G = PermutationGroup([[(1,2),(3,4)], [(1,2,3)]])
sage: latex(G.character_table())
\left(\begin{array}{rrrr}
1 & 1 & 1 & 1 \\
1 & 1 & -\zeta_{3} - 1 & \zeta_{3} \\
1 & 1 & \zeta_{3} & -\zeta_{3} - 1 \\
3 & -1 & 0 & 0
\end{array}\right)
```

Sage also includes classical and matrix groups over finite fields:

```
sage: MS = MatrixSpace(GF(7), 2)
sage: gens = [MS([[1,0],[-1,1]]),MS([[1,1],[0,1]])]
sage: G = MatrixGroup(gens)
sage: G.conjugacy_class_representatives()
(
[1 0]  [0 1]  [0 1]  [0 1]  [0 1]  [0 1]  [0 1]  [0 3]  [0 3]  [0 1]
[0 1], [6 1], [6 3], [6 2], [6 6], [6 4], [6 5], [2 2], [2 5], [6 0],

[6 0]
[0 6]
)
sage: G = Sp(4,GF(7))
sage: G
Symplectic Group of degree 4 over Finite Field of size 7
sage: G.random_element()                # random output
[5 5 5 1]
[0 2 6 3]
[5 0 1 0]
[4 6 3 4]
sage: G.order()
276595200
```

You can also compute using abelian groups (infinite and finite):

```
sage: F = AbelianGroup(5, [5,5,7,8,9], names='abcde')
sage: (a, b, c, d, e) = F.gens()
sage: d * b**2 * c**3
b^2*c^3*d
sage: F = AbelianGroup(3,[2]*3); F
```

2.11. Finite Groups, Abelian Groups

```
Multiplicative Abelian group isomorphic to C2 x C2 x C2
sage: H = AbelianGroup([2,3], names="xy"); H
Multiplicative Abelian group isomorphic to C2 x C3
sage: AbelianGroup(5)
Multiplicative Abelian group isomorphic to Z x Z x Z x Z x Z
sage: AbelianGroup(5).order()
+Infinity
```

2.12 Number Theory

Sage has extensive functionality for number theory. For example, we can do arithmetic in $\mathbf{Z}/N\mathbf{Z}$ as follows:

```
sage: R = IntegerModRing(97)
sage: a = R(2) / R(3)
sage: a
33
sage: a.rational_reconstruction()
2/3
sage: b = R(47)
sage: b^20052005
50
sage: b.modulus()
97
sage: b.is_square()
True
```

Sage contains standard number theoretic functions. For example,

```
sage: gcd(515,2005)
5
sage: factor(2005)
5 * 401
sage: c = factorial(25); c
15511210043330985984000000
sage: [valuation(c,p) for p in prime_range(2,23)]
[22, 10, 6, 3, 2, 1, 1, 1]
sage: next_prime(2005)
2011
sage: previous_prime(2005)
2003
sage: divisors(28); sum(divisors(28)); 2*28
[1, 2, 4, 7, 14, 28]
56
56
```

Perfect!

Sage's `sigma(n,k)` function adds up the kth powers of the divisors of n:

```
sage: sigma(28,0); sigma(28,1); sigma(28,2)
6
56
1050
```

We next illustrate the extended Euclidean algorithm, Euler's ϕ-function, and the Chinese remainder theorem:

```
sage: d,u,v = xgcd(12,15)
sage: d == u*12 + v*15
True
sage: n = 2005
sage: inverse_mod(3,n)
1337
sage: 3 * 1337
4011
sage: prime_divisors(n)
[5, 401]
sage: phi = n*prod([1 - 1/p for p in prime_divisors(n)]); phi
1600
sage: euler_phi(n)
1600
sage: prime_to_m_part(n, 5)
401
```

We next verify something about the $3n + 1$ problem.

```
sage: n = 2005
sage: for i in range(1000):
...       n = 3*odd_part(n) + 1
...       if odd_part(n)==1:
...           print i
...           break
38
```

Finally we illustrate the Chinese remainder theorem.

```
sage: x = crt(2, 1, 3, 5); x
11
sage: x % 3    # x mod 3 = 2
2
sage: x % 5    # x mod 5 = 1
1
sage: [binomial(13,m) for m in range(14)]
[1, 13, 78, 286, 715, 1287, 1716, 1716, 1287, 715, 286, 78, 13, 1]
sage: [binomial(13,m)%2 for m in range(14)]
[1, 1, 0, 0, 1, 1, 0, 0, 1, 1, 0, 0, 1, 1]
sage: [kronecker(m,13) for m in range(1,13)]
[1, -1, 1, 1, -1, -1, -1, -1, 1, 1, -1, 1]
sage: n = 10000; sum([moebius(m) for m in range(1,n)])
-23
sage: Partitions(4).list()
[[4], [3, 1], [2, 2], [2, 1, 1], [1, 1, 1, 1]]
```

2.12.1 p-adic Numbers

The field of p-adic numbers is implemented in Sage. Note that once a p-adic field is created, you cannot change its precision.

```
sage: K = Qp(11); K
11-adic Field with capped relative precision 20
sage: a = K(211/17); a
4 + 4*11 + 11^2 + 7*11^3 + 9*11^5 + 5*11^6 + 4*11^7 + 8*11^8 + 7*11^9
  + 9*11^10 + 3*11^11 + 10*11^12 + 11^13 + 5*11^14 + 6*11^15 + 2*11^16
  + 3*11^17 + 11^18 + 7*11^19 + O(11^20)
sage: b = K(3211/11^2); b
10*11^-2 + 5*11^-1 + 4 + 2*11 + O(11^18)
```

Much work has been done implementing rings of integers in p-adic fields or number fields other than . The interested reader is invited to ask the experts on the `sage-support` Google group for further details.

A number of related methods are already implemented in the NumberField class.

```
sage: R.<x> = PolynomialRing(QQ)
sage: K = NumberField(x^3 + x^2 - 2*x + 8, 'a')
sage: K.integral_basis()
[1, 1/2*a^2 + 1/2*a, a^2]
```

```
sage: K.galois_group(type="pari")
Galois group PARI group [6, -1, 2, "S3"] of degree 3 of the Number Field
in a with defining polynomial x^3 + x^2 - 2*x + 8
```

```
sage: K.polynomial_quotient_ring()
Univariate Quotient Polynomial Ring in a over Rational Field with modulus
x^3 + x^2 - 2*x + 8
sage: K.units()
[3*a^2 + 13*a + 13]
sage: K.discriminant()
-503
sage: K.class_group()
Class group of order 1 of Number Field in a with
defining polynomial x^3 + x^2 - 2*x + 8
sage: K.class_number()
1
```

2.13 Some More Advanced Mathematics

2.13.1 Algebraic Geometry

You can define arbitrary algebraic varieties in Sage, but sometimes nontrivial functionality is limited to rings over **Q** or finite fields. For example, we compute the union of two affine plane curves, then recover the curves as the irreducible components of the union.

```
sage: x, y = AffineSpace(2, QQ, 'xy').gens()
sage: C2 = Curve(x^2 + y^2 - 1)
sage: C3 = Curve(x^3 + y^3 - 1)
sage: D = C2 + C3
sage: D
Affine Curve over Rational Field defined by
  x^5 + x^3*y^2 + x^2*y^3 + y^5 - x^3 - y^3 - x^2 - y^2 + 1
sage: D.irreducible_components()
[
Closed subscheme of Affine Space of dimension 2 over Rational Field defined by:
  x^2 + y^2 - 1,
Closed subscheme of Affine Space of dimension 2 over Rational Field defined by:
  x^3 + y^3 - 1
]
```

We can also find all points of intersection of the two curves by intersecting them and computing the irreducible components.

```
sage: V = C2.intersection(C3)
sage: V.irreducible_components()
[
Closed subscheme of Affine Space of dimension 2 over Rational Field defined by:
  y - 1,
  x,
Closed subscheme of Affine Space of dimension 2 over Rational Field defined by:
  y,
  x - 1,
Closed subscheme of Affine Space of dimension 2 over Rational Field defined by:
  x + y + 2,
  2*y^2 + 4*y + 3
]
```

Thus, e.g., $(1, 0)$ and $(0, 1)$ are on both curves (visibly clear), as are certain (quadratic) points whose y coordinates satisfy $2y^2 + 4y + 3 = 0$.

Sage can compute the toric ideal of the twisted cubic in projective 3 space:

```
sage: R.<a,b,c,d> = PolynomialRing(QQ, 4)
sage: I = ideal(b^2-a*c, c^2-b*d, a*d-b*c)
sage: F = I.groebner_fan(); F
Groebner fan of the ideal:
Ideal (b^2 - a*c, c^2 - b*d, -b*c + a*d) of Multivariate Polynomial Ring
in a, b, c, d over Rational Field
sage: F.reduced_groebner_bases ()
[[-c^2 + b*d, -b*c + a*d, -b^2 + a*c],
 [-c^2 + b*d, b^2 - a*c, -b*c + a*d],
 [-c^2 + b*d, b*c - a*d, b^2 - a*c, -c^3 + a*d^2],
 [c^3 - a*d^2, -c^2 + b*d, b*c - a*d, b^2 - a*c],
 [c^2 - b*d, -b*c + a*d, -b^2 + a*c],
 [c^2 - b*d, b*c - a*d, -b^2 + a*c, -b^3 + a^2*d],
 [c^2 - b*d, b*c - a*d, b^3 - a^2*d, -b^2 + a*c],
 [c^2 - b*d, b*c - a*d, b^2 - a*c]]
```

```
sage: F.polyhedralfan()
Polyhedral fan in 4 dimensions of dimension 4
```

2.13.2 Elliptic Curves

Elliptic curve functionality includes most of the elliptic curve functionality of PARI, access to the data in Cremona's online tables (this requires an optional database package), the functionality of mwrank, i.e., 2-descents with computation of the full Mordell-Weil group, the SEA algorithm, computation of all isogenies, much new code for curves over **Q**, and some of Denis Simon's algebraic descent software.

The command `EllipticCurve` for creating an elliptic curve has many forms:

- EllipticCurve($[a_1, a_2, a_3, a_4, a_6]$): Returns the elliptic curve

$$y^2 + a_1 xy + a_3 y = x^3 + a_2 x^2 + a_4 x + a_6,$$

  where the a_i's are coerced into the parent of a_1. If all the a_i have parent **Z**, they are coerced into **Q**.

- EllipticCurve($[a_4, a_6]$): Same as above, but $a_1 = a_2 = a_3 = 0$.

- EllipticCurve(label): Returns the elliptic curve over from the Cremona database with the given (new!) Cremona label. The label is a string, such as `"11a"` or `"37b2"`. The letter must be lower case (to distinguish it from the old labeling).

- EllipticCurve(j): Returns an elliptic curve with j-invariant j.

- EllipticCurve(R, $[a_1, a_2, a_3, a_4, a_6]$): Create the elliptic curve over a ring R with given a_i's as above.

We illustrate each of these constructors:

```
sage: EllipticCurve([0,0,1,-1,0])
Elliptic Curve defined by y^2 + y = x^3 - x over Rational Field

sage: EllipticCurve([GF(5)(0),0,1,-1,0])
Elliptic Curve defined by y^2 + y = x^3 + 4*x over Finite Field of size 5

sage: EllipticCurve([1,2])
Elliptic Curve defined by y^2  = x^3 + x + 2 over Rational Field

sage: EllipticCurve('37a')
Elliptic Curve defined by y^2 + y = x^3 - x over Rational Field

sage: EllipticCurve_from_j(1)
Elliptic Curve defined by y^2 + x*y = x^3 + 36*x + 3455 over Rational Field

sage: EllipticCurve(GF(5), [0,0,1,-1,0])
Elliptic Curve defined by y^2 + y = x^3 + 4*x over Finite Field of size 5
```

The pair $(0,0)$ is a point on the elliptic curve E defined by $y^2 + y = x^3 - x$. To create this point in Sage type `E([0,0])`. Sage can add points on such an elliptic curve (recall elliptic curves support an additive group structure where the point at infinity is the zero element and three co-linear points on the curve add to zero):

```
sage: E = EllipticCurve([0,0,1,-1,0])
sage: E
Elliptic Curve defined by y^2 + y = x^3 - x over Rational Field
sage: P = E([0,0])
sage: P + P
(1 : 0 : 1)
sage: 10*P
(161/16 : -2065/64 : 1)
sage: 20*P
(683916417/264517696 : -18784454671297/4302115807744 : 1)
sage: E.conductor()
37
```

The elliptic curves over the complex numbers are parameterized by the j-invariant. Sage computes j-invariant as follows:

```
sage: E = EllipticCurve([0,0,0,-4,2]); E
Elliptic Curve defined by y^2 = x^3 - 4*x + 2 over Rational Field
sage: E.conductor()
2368
sage: E.j_invariant()
110592/37
```

If we make a curve with the same j-invariant as that of E, it need not be isomorphic to E. In the following example, the curves are not isomorphic because their conductors are different.

```
sage: F = EllipticCurve_from_j(110592/37)
sage: F.conductor()
37
```

However, the twist of F by 2 gives an isomorphic curve.

```
sage: G = F.quadratic_twist(2); G
Elliptic Curve defined by y^2 = x^3 - 4*x + 2 over Rational Field
sage: G.conductor()
2368
sage: G.j_invariant()
110592/37
```

We can compute the coefficients a_n of the L-series or modular form $\sum_{n=0}^{\infty} a_n q^n$ attached to the elliptic curve. This computation uses the PARI C-library:

```
sage: E = EllipticCurve([0,0,1,-1,0])
sage: print E.anlist(30)
[0, 1, -2, -3, 2, -2, 6, -1, 0, 6, 4, -5, -6, -2, 2, 6, -4, 0, -12, 0, -4,
 3, 10, 2, 0, -1, 4, -9, -2, 6, -12]
sage: v = E.anlist(10000)
```

It only takes a second to compute all a_n for $n \leq 10^5$:

```
sage: %time v = E.anlist(100000)
CPU times: user 0.98 s, sys: 0.06 s, total: 1.04 s
Wall time: 1.06
```

2.13. Some More Advanced Mathematics

Elliptic curves can be constructed using their Cremona labels. This pre-loads the elliptic curve with information about its rank, Tamagawa numbers, regulator, etc.

```
sage: E = EllipticCurve("37b2")
sage: E
Elliptic Curve defined by y^2 + y = x^3 + x^2 - 1873*x - 31833 over Rational
Field
sage: E = EllipticCurve("389a")
sage: E
Elliptic Curve defined by y^2 + y = x^3 + x^2 - 2*x  over Rational Field
sage: E.rank()
2
sage: E = EllipticCurve("5077a")
sage: E.rank()
3
```

We can also access the Cremona database directly.

```
sage: db = sage.databases.cremona.CremonaDatabase()
sage: db.curves(37)
{'a1': [[0, 0, 1, -1, 0], 1, 1], 'b1': [[0, 1, 1, -23, -50], 0, 3]}
sage: db.allcurves(37)
{'a1': [[0, 0, 1, -1, 0], 1, 1],
 'b1': [[0, 1, 1, -23, -50], 0, 3],
 'b2': [[0, 1, 1, -1873, -31833], 0, 1],
 'b3': [[0, 1, 1, -3, 1], 0, 3]}
```

The objects returned from the database are not of type `EllipticCurve`. They are elements of a database and have a couple of fields, and that's it. There is a small version of Cremona's database, which is distributed by default with Sage, and contains limited information about elliptic curves of conductor ≤ 10000. There is also a large optional version, which contains extensive data about all curves of conductor up to 120000 (as of October 2005). There is also a huge (2GB) optional database package for Sage that contains the hundreds of millions of elliptic curves in the Stein-Watkins database.

2.13.3 Dirichlet Characters

A *Dirichlet character* is the extension of a homomorphism $(\mathbf{Z}/N\mathbf{Z})^* \to R^*$, for some ring R, to the map $\mathbf{Z} \to R$ obtained by sending those integers x with $\gcd(N, x) > 1$ to 0.

```
sage: G = DirichletGroup(12)
sage: G.list()
[Dirichlet character modulo 12 of conductor 1 mapping 7 |--> 1, 5 |--> 1,
Dirichlet character modulo 12 of conductor 4 mapping 7 |--> -1, 5 |--> 1,
Dirichlet character modulo 12 of conductor 3 mapping 7 |--> 1, 5 |--> -1,
Dirichlet character modulo 12 of conductor 12 mapping 7 |--> -1, 5 |--> -1]
sage: G.gens()
(Dirichlet character modulo 12 of conductor 4 mapping 7 |--> -1, 5 |--> 1,
Dirichlet character modulo 12 of conductor 3 mapping 7 |--> 1, 5 |--> -1)
sage: len(G)
4
```

Having created the group, we next create an element and compute with it.

```
sage: G = DirichletGroup(21)
sage: chi = G.1; chi
Dirichlet character modulo 21 of conductor 7 mapping 8 |--> 1, 10 |--> zeta6
sage: chi.values()
[0, 1, zeta6 - 1, 0, -zeta6, -zeta6 + 1, 0, 0, 1, 0, zeta6, -zeta6, 0, -1,
 0, 0, zeta6 - 1, zeta6, 0, -zeta6 + 1, -1]
sage: chi.conductor()
7
sage: chi.modulus()
21
sage: chi.order()
6
sage: chi(19)
-zeta6 + 1
sage: chi(40)
-zeta6 + 1
```

It is also possible to compute the action of the Galois group $\mathrm{Gal}(\mathbf{Q}(\zeta_N)/\mathbf{Q})$ on these characters, as well as the direct product decomposition corresponding to the factorization of the modulus.

```
sage: chi.galois_orbit()
[Dirichlet character modulo 21 of conductor 7 mapping 8 |--> 1, 10 |--> zeta6,
Dirichlet character modulo 21 of conductor 7 mapping 8 |--> 1, 10 |--> -zeta6 + 1]

sage: go = G.galois_orbits()
sage: [len(orbit) for orbit in go]
[1, 2, 2, 1, 1, 2, 2, 1]

sage: G.decomposition()
[
Group of Dirichlet characters of modulus 3 over Cyclotomic Field of order
6 and degree 2,
Group of Dirichlet characters of modulus 7 over Cyclotomic Field of order
6 and degree 2
]
```

Next, we construct the group of Dirichlet characters mod 20, but with values in $\mathbf{Q}(i)$:

```
sage: K.<i> = NumberField(x^2+1)
sage: G = DirichletGroup(20,K)
sage: G
Group of [...] of modulus 20 over Number Field in i with defining polynomial x^2 + 1
```

We next compute several invariants of G:

```
sage: G.gens()
(Dirichlet character modulo 20 of conductor 4 mapping 11 |--> -1, 17 |--> 1,
Dirichlet character modulo 20 of conductor 5 mapping 11 |--> 1, 17 |--> -i)

sage: G.unit_gens()
(11, 17)
sage: G.zeta()
-i
```

```
sage: G.zeta_order()
4
```

In this example we create a Dirichlet character with values in a number field. We explicitly specify the choice of root of unity by the third argument to `DirichletGroup` below.

```
sage: x = polygen(QQ, 'x')
sage: K = NumberField(x^4 + 1, 'a'); a = K.0
sage: b = K.gen(); a == b
True
sage: K
Number Field in a with defining polynomial x^4 + 1
sage: G = DirichletGroup(5, K, a); G
Group of Dirichlet characters of modulus 5 over Number Field in a with
defining polynomial x^4 + 1
sage: chi = G.0; chi
Dirichlet character modulo 5 of conductor 5 mapping 2 |--> a^2
sage: [(chi^i)(2) for i in range(4)]
[1, a^2, -1, -a^2]
```

Here `NumberField(x^4 + 1, 'a')` tells Sage to use the symbol "a" in printing what K is (a Number Field in a with defining polynomial $x^4 + 1$). The name "a" is undeclared at this point. Once `a = K.0` (or equivalently `a = K.gen()`) is evaluated, the symbol "a" represents a root of the generating polynomial $x^4 + 1$.

2.13.4 Modular Forms

Sage can do some computations related to modular forms, including dimensions, computing spaces of modular symbols, Hecke operators, and decompositions.

There are several functions available for computing dimensions of spaces of modular forms. For example,

```
sage: dimension_cusp_forms(Gamma0(11),2)
1
sage: dimension_cusp_forms(Gamma0(1),12)
1
sage: dimension_cusp_forms(Gamma1(389),2)
6112
```

Next we illustrate computation of Hecke operators on a space of modular symbols of level 1 and weight 12.

```
sage: M = ModularSymbols(1,12)
sage: M.basis()
([X^8*Y^2,(0,0)], [X^9*Y,(0,0)], [X^10,(0,0)])
sage: t2 = M.T(2)
sage: t2
Hecke operator T_2 on Modular Symbols space of dimension 3 for Gamma_0(1)
of weight 12 with sign 0 over Rational Field
sage: t2.matrix()
[ -24    0    0]
[   0  -24    0]
```

```
[4860    0 2049]
sage: f = t2.charpoly('x'); f
x^3 - 2001*x^2 - 97776*x - 1180224
sage: factor(f)
(x - 2049) * (x + 24)^2
sage: M.T(11).charpoly('x').factor()
(x - 285311670612) * (x - 534612)^2
```

We can also create spaces for $\Gamma_0(N)$ and $\Gamma_1(N)$.

```
sage: ModularSymbols(11,2)
Modular Symbols space of dimension 3 for Gamma_0(11) of weight 2 with sign
 0 over Rational Field
sage: ModularSymbols(Gamma1(11),2)
Modular Symbols space of dimension 11 for Gamma_1(11) of weight 2 with
sign 0 and over Rational Field
```

Let's compute some characteristic polynomials and q-expansions.

```
sage: M = ModularSymbols(Gamma1(11),2)
sage: M.T(2).charpoly('x')
x^11 - 8*x^10 + 20*x^9 + 10*x^8 - 145*x^7 + 229*x^6 + 58*x^5 - 360*x^4
    + 70*x^3 - 515*x^2 + 1804*x - 1452
sage: M.T(2).charpoly('x').factor()
(x - 3) * (x + 2)^2 * (x^4 - 7*x^3 + 19*x^2 - 23*x + 11)
        * (x^4 - 2*x^3 + 4*x^2 + 2*x + 11)
sage: S = M.cuspidal_submodule()
sage: S.T(2).matrix()
[-2  0]
[ 0 -2]
sage: S.q_expansion_basis(10)
[
    q - 2*q^2 - q^3 + 2*q^4 + q^5 + 2*q^6 - 2*q^7 - 2*q^9 + O(q^10)
]
```

We can even compute spaces of modular symbols with character.

```
sage: G = DirichletGroup(13)
sage: e = G.0^2
sage: M = ModularSymbols(e,2); M
Modular Symbols space of dimension 4 and level 13, weight 2, character
[zeta6], sign 0, over Cyclotomic Field of order 6 and degree 2
sage: M.T(2).charpoly('x').factor()
(x - zeta6 - 2) * (x - 2*zeta6 - 1) * (x + zeta6 + 1)^2
sage: S = M.cuspidal_submodule(); S
Modular Symbols subspace of dimension 2 of Modular Symbols space of
dimension 4 and level 13, weight 2, character [zeta6], sign 0, over
Cyclotomic Field of order 6 and degree 2
sage: S.T(2).charpoly('x').factor()
(x + zeta6 + 1)^2
sage: S.q_expansion_basis(10)
[
q + (-zeta6 - 1)*q^2 + (2*zeta6 - 2)*q^3 + zeta6*q^4 + (-2*zeta6 + 1)*q^5
```

```
        + (-2*zeta6 + 4)*q^6 + (2*zeta6 - 1)*q^8 - zeta6*q^9 + O(q^10)
]
```

Here is another example of how Sage can compute the action of Hecke operators on a space of modular forms.

```
sage: T = ModularForms(Gamma0(11),2)
sage: T
Modular Forms space of dimension 2 for Congruence Subgroup Gamma0(11) of
weight 2 over Rational Field
sage: T.degree()
2
sage: T.level()
11
sage: T.group()
Congruence Subgroup Gamma0(11)
sage: T.dimension()
2
sage: T.cuspidal_subspace()
Cuspidal subspace of dimension 1 of Modular Forms space of dimension 2 for
Congruence Subgroup Gamma0(11) of weight 2 over Rational Field
sage: T.eisenstein_subspace()
Eisenstein subspace of dimension 1 of Modular Forms space of dimension 2
for Congruence Subgroup Gamma0(11) of weight 2 over Rational Field
sage: M = ModularSymbols(11); M
Modular Symbols space of dimension 3 for Gamma_0(11) of weight 2 with sign
0 over Rational Field
sage: M.weight()
2
sage: M.basis()
((1,0), (1,8), (1,9))
sage: M.sign()
0
```

Let T_p denote the usual Hecke operators (p prime). How do the Hecke operators T_2, T_3, T_5 act on the space of modular symbols?

```
sage: M.T(2).matrix()
[ 3  0 -1]
[ 0 -2  0]
[ 0  0 -2]
sage: M.T(3).matrix()
[ 4  0 -1]
[ 0 -1  0]
[ 0  0 -1]
sage: M.T(5).matrix()
[ 6  0 -1]
[ 0  1  0]
[ 0  0  1]
```

CHAPTER
THREE

THE INTERACTIVE SHELL

In most of this tutorial, we assume you start the Sage interpreter using the `sage` command. This starts a customized version of the IPython shell, and imports many functions and classes, so they are ready to use from the command prompt. Further customization is possible by editing the `$SAGE_ROOT/ipythonrc` file. Upon starting Sage, you get output similar to the following:

```
----------------------------------------------------------------
| SAGE Version 3.1.1, Release Date: 2008-05-24                 |
| Type notebook() for the GUI, and license() for information.  |
----------------------------------------------------------------

sage:
```

To quit Sage either press Ctrl-D or type `quit` or `exit`.

```
sage: quit
Exiting SAGE (CPU time 0m0.00s, Wall time 0m0.89s)
```

The wall time is the time that elapsed on the clock hanging from your wall. This is relevant, since CPU time does not track time used by subprocesses like GAP or Singular.

(Avoid killing a Sage process with `kill -9` from a terminal, since Sage might not kill child processes, e.g., Maple processes, or cleanup temporary files from `$HOME/.sage/tmp`.)

3.1 Your Sage Session

The session is the sequence of input and output from when you start Sage until you quit. Sage logs all Sage input, via IPython. In fact, if you're using the interactive shell (not the notebook interface), then at any point you may type `%history` (or `%hist`) to get a listing of all input lines typed so far. You can type `?` at the Sage prompt to find out more about IPython, e.g., "IPython offers numbered prompts ... with input and output caching. All input is saved and can be retrieved as variables (besides the usual arrow key recall). The following GLOBAL variables always exist (so don't overwrite them!)":

```
_:   previous input (interactive shell and notebook)
__:  next previous input (interactive shell only)
_oh : list of all inputs (interactive shell only)
```

Here is an example:

```
sage: factor(100)
 _1 = 2^2 * 5^2
sage: kronecker_symbol(3,5)
 _2 = -1
sage: %hist     #This only works from the interactive shell, not the notebook.
1: factor(100)
2: kronecker_symbol(3,5)
3: %hist
sage: _oh
 _4 = {1: 2^2 * 5^2, 2: -1}
sage: _i1
 _5 = 'factor(ZZ(100))\n'
sage: eval(_i1)
 _6 = 2^2 * 5^2
sage: %hist
1: factor(100)
2: kronecker_symbol(3,5)
3: %hist
4: _oh
5: _i1
6: eval(_i1)
7: %hist
```

We omit the output numbering in the rest of this tutorial and the other Sage documentation.

You can also store a list of input from session in a macro for that session.

```
sage: E = EllipticCurve([1,2,3,4,5])
sage: M = ModularSymbols(37)
sage: %hist
1: E = EllipticCurve([1,2,3,4,5])
2: M = ModularSymbols(37)
3: %hist
sage: %macro em 1-2
Macro `em` created. To execute, type its name (without quotes).

sage: E
Elliptic Curve defined by y^2 + x*y + 3*y = x^3 + 2*x^2 + 4*x + 5 over
Rational Field
sage: E = 5
sage: M = None
sage: em
Executing Macro...
sage: E
Elliptic Curve defined by y^2 + x*y + 3*y = x^3 + 2*x^2 + 4*x + 5 over
Rational Field
```

When using the interactive shell, any UNIX shell command can be executed from Sage by prefacing it by an exclamation point !. For example,

```
sage: !ls
auto   example.sage  glossary.tex   t   tmp   tut.log   tut.tex
```

returns the listing of the current directory.

The `PATH` has the Sage bin directory at the front, so if you run `gp`, `gap`, `singular`, `maxima`, etc., you get the versions included with Sage.

```
sage: !gp
Reading GPRC: /etc/gprc ...Done.

                    GP/PARI CALCULATOR Version 2.2.11 (alpha)
              i686 running linux (ix86/GMP-4.1.4 kernel) 32-bit version
...
sage: !singular
                    SINGULAR                       /  Development
 A Computer Algebra System for Polynomial Computations   /   version 3-0-1
                                                    0<
     by: G.-M. Greuel, G. Pfister, H. Schoenemann     \   October 2005
FB Mathematik der Universitaet, D-67653 Kaiserslautern  \
```

3.2 Logging Input and Output

Logging your Sage session is not the same as saving it (see *Saving and Loading Complete Sessions* for that). To log input (and optionally output) use the `logstart` command. Type `logstart?` for more details. You can use this command to log all input you type, all output, and even play back that input in a future session (by simply reloading the log file).

```
was@form:~$ sage
----------------------------------------------------------------------
| SAGE Version 3.0.2, Release Date: 2008-05-24                       |
| Type notebook() for the GUI, and license() for information.        |
----------------------------------------------------------------------

sage: logstart setup
Activating auto-logging. Current session state plus future input saved.
Filename       : setup
Mode           : backup
Output logging : False
Timestamping   : False
State          : active
sage: E = EllipticCurve([1,2,3,4,5]).minimal_model()
sage: F = QQ^3
sage: x,y = QQ['x,y'].gens()
sage: G = E.gens()
sage:
Exiting SAGE (CPU time 0m0.61s, Wall time 0m50.39s).
```

```
was@form:~$ sage
----------------------------------------------------------------------
| SAGE Version 3.0.2, Release Date: 2008-05-24                       |
| Type notebook() for the GUI, and license() for information.        |
----------------------------------------------------------------------
sage: load "setup"
Loading log file <setup> one line at a time...
Finished replaying log file <setup>
sage: E
Elliptic Curve defined by y^2 + x*y  = x^3 - x^2 + 4*x + 3 over Rational
Field
sage: x*y
x*y
sage: G
[(2 : 3 : 1)]
```

If you use Sage in the Linux KDE terminal `konsole` then you can save your session as follows: after starting Sage in `konsole`, select "settings", then "history...", then "set unlimited". When you are ready to save your session, select "edit" then "save history as..." and type in a name to save the text of your session to your computer. After saving this file, you could then load it into an editor, such as xemacs, and print it.

3.3 Paste Ignores Prompts

Suppose you are reading a session of Sage or Python computations and want to copy them into Sage. But there are annoying >>> or `sage:` prompts to worry about. In fact, you can copy and paste an example, including the prompts if you want, into Sage. In other words, by default the Sage parser strips any leading >>> or `sage:` prompt before passing it to Python. For example,

```
sage: 2^10
1024
sage: sage: sage: 2^10
1024
sage: >>> 2^10
1024
```

3.4 Timing Commands

If you place the `%time` command at the beginning of an input line, the time the command takes to run will be displayed after the output. For example, we can compare the running time for a certain exponentiation operation in several ways. The timings below will probably be much different on your computer, or even between different versions of Sage. First, native Python:

```
sage: %time a = int(1938)^int(99484)
CPU times: user 0.66 s, sys: 0.00 s, total: 0.66 s
Wall time: 0.66
```

This means that 0.66 seconds total were taken, and the "Wall time", i.e., the amount of time that elapsed on your wall clock, is also 0.66 seconds. If your computer is heavily loaded with other programs, the wall time may be much larger than the CPU time.

Next we time exponentiation using the native Sage Integer type, which is implemented (in Cython) using the GMP library:

```
sage: %time a = 1938^99484
CPU times: user 0.04 s, sys: 0.00 s, total: 0.04 s
Wall time: 0.04
```

Using the PARI C-library interface:

```
sage: %time a = pari(1938)^pari(99484)
CPU times: user 0.05 s, sys: 0.00 s, total: 0.05 s
Wall time: 0.05
```

GMP is better, but only slightly (as expected, since the version of PARI built for Sage uses GMP for integer arithmetic).

You can also time a block of commands using the `cputime` command, as illustrated below:

```
sage: t = cputime()
sage: a = int(1938)^int(99484)
sage: b = 1938^99484
sage: c = pari(1938)^pari(99484)
sage: cputime(t)                    # somewhat random output
0.64

sage: cputime?
...
    Return the time in CPU second since SAGE started, or with optional
    argument t, return the time since time t.
    INPUT:
        t -- (optional) float, time in CPU seconds
    OUTPUT:
        float -- time in CPU seconds
```

The `walltime` command behaves just like the `cputime` command, except that it measures wall time.

We can also compute the above power in some of the computer algebra systems that Sage includes. In each case we execute a trivial command in the system, in order to start up the server for that program. The most relevant time is the wall time. However, if there is a significant difference between the wall time and the CPU time then this may indicate a performance issue worth looking into.

```
sage: time 1938^99484;
CPU times: user 0.01 s, sys: 0.00 s, total: 0.01 s
Wall time: 0.01
sage: gp(0)
0
sage: time g = gp('1938^99484')
CPU times: user 0.00 s, sys: 0.00 s, total: 0.00 s
Wall time: 0.04
sage: maxima(0)
```

```
0
sage: time g = maxima('1938^99484')
CPU times: user 0.00 s, sys: 0.00 s, total: 0.00 s
Wall time: 0.30
sage: kash(0)
0
sage: time g = kash('1938^99484')
CPU times: user 0.00 s, sys: 0.00 s, total: 0.00 s
Wall time: 0.04
sage: mathematica(0)
        0
sage: time g = mathematica('1938^99484')
CPU times: user 0.00 s, sys: 0.00 s, total: 0.00 s
Wall time: 0.03
sage: maple(0)
0
sage: time g = maple('1938^99484')
CPU times: user 0.00 s, sys: 0.00 s, total: 0.00 s
Wall time: 0.11
sage: gap(0)
0
sage: time g = gap.eval('1938^99484;;')
CPU times: user 0.00 s, sys: 0.00 s, total: 0.00 s
Wall time: 1.02
```

Note that GAP and Maxima are the slowest in this test (this was run on the machine `sage.math.washington.edu`). Because of the pexpect interface overhead, it is perhaps unfair to compare these to Sage, which is the fastest.

3.5 Other IPython tricks

As noted above, Sage uses IPython as its front end, and so you can use any of IPython's commands and features. You can read the full IPython documentation. Meanwhile, here are some fun tricks – these are called "Magic commands" in IPython:

- You can use `%bg` to run a command in the background, and then use `jobs` to access the results, as follows. (The comments `not tested` are here because the `%bg` syntax doesn't work well with Sage's automatic testing facility. If you type this in yourself, it should work as written. This is of course most useful with commands which take a while to complete.)

    ```
    sage: def quick(m): return 2*m
    sage: %bg quick(20)     # not tested
    Starting job # 0 in a separate thread.
    sage: jobs.status()     # not tested
    Completed jobs:
    0 : quick(20)
    sage: jobs[0].result    # the actual answer, not tested
    40
    ```

    Note that jobs run in the background don't use the Sage preparser – see *The Pre-Parser: Differences between Sage and Python* for more information. One (perhaps awkward) way to get around this would be to run

```
sage: %bg eval(preparse('quick(20)'))   # not tested
```

It is safer and easier, though, to just use `%bg` on commands which don't require the preparser.

- You can use `%edit` (or `%ed` or `ed`) to open an editor, if you want to type in some complex code. Before you start Sage, make sure that the `EDITOR` environment variable is set to your favorite editor (by putting `export EDITOR=/usr/bin/emacs` or `export EDITOR=/usr/bin/vim` or something similar in the appropriate place, like a `.profile` file). From the Sage prompt, executing `%edit` will open up the named editor. Then within the editor you can define a function:

```
def some_function(n):
    return n**2 + 3*n + 2
```

Save and quit from the editor. For the rest of your Sage session, you can then use `some_function`. If you want to modify it, type `%edit some_function` from the Sage prompt.

- If you have a computation and you want to modify its output for another use, perform the computation and type `%rep`: this will place the output from the previous command at the Sage prompt, ready for you to edit it.

```
sage: f(x) = cos(x)
sage: f(x).derivative(x)
-sin(x)
```

At this point, if you type `%rep` at the Sage prompt, you will get a new Sage prompt, followed by `-sin(x)`, with the cursor at the end of the line.

For more, type `%quickref` to get a quick reference guide to IPython. As of this writing (April 2011), Sage uses version 0.9.1 of IPython, and the documentation for its magic commands is available online. Various slightly advanced aspects of magic command system are documented here in IPython.

3.6 Errors and Exceptions

When something goes wrong, you will usually see a Python "exception". Python even tries to suggest what raised the exception. Often you see the name of the exception, e.g., `NameError` or `ValueError` (see the Python Reference Manual [Py] for a complete list of exceptions). For example,

```
sage: 3_2
------------------------------------------------------------
   File "<console>", line 1
     ZZ(3)_2
          ^
SyntaxError: invalid syntax

sage: EllipticCurve([0,infinity])
------------------------------------------------------------
Traceback (most recent call last):
```

```
...
TypeError: Unable to coerce Infinity (<class 'sage...Infinity'>) to Rational
```

The interactive debugger is sometimes useful for understanding what went wrong. You can toggle it on or off using `%pdb` (the default is off). The prompt `ipdb>` appears if an exception is raised and the debugger is on. From within the debugger, you can print the state of any local variable, and move up and down the execution stack. For example,

```
sage: %pdb
Automatic pdb calling has been turned ON
sage: EllipticCurve([1,infinity])
------------------------------------------------------------
<type 'exceptions.TypeError'>         Traceback (most recent call last)
...

ipdb>
```

For a list of commands in the debugger, type ? at the `ipdb>` prompt:

```
ipdb> ?

Documented commands (type help <topic>):
========================================
EOF     break    commands    debug    h       l      pdef    quit    tbreak
a       bt       condition   disable  help    list   pdoc    r       u
alias   c        cont        down     ignore  n      pinfo   return  unalias
args    cl       continue    enable   j       next   pp      s       up
b       clear    d           exit     jump    p      q       step    w
whatis  where

Miscellaneous help topics:
==========================
exec  pdb

Undocumented commands:
======================
retval  rv
```

Type Ctrl-D or `quit` to return to Sage.

3.7 Reverse Search and Tab Completion

Reverse search: Type the beginning of a command, then `Ctrl-p` (or just hit the up arrow key) to go back to each line you have entered that begins in that way. This works even if you completely exit Sage and restart later. You can also do a reverse search through the history using `Ctrl-r`. All these features use the `readline` package, which is available on most flavors of Linux.

To illustrate tab completion, first create the three dimensional vector space $V = \mathbf{Q}^3$ as follows:

```
sage: V = VectorSpace(QQ,3)
sage: V
Vector space of dimension 3 over Rational Field
```

You can also use the following more concise notation:

```
sage: V = QQ^3
```

Then it is easy to list all member functions for V using tab completion. Just type V., then type the [tab key] key on your keyboard:

```
sage: V.[tab key]
V._VectorSpace_generic__base_field
...
V.ambient_space
V.base_field
V.base_ring
V.basis
V.coordinates
...
V.zero_vector
```

If you type the first few letters of a function, then [tab key], you get only functions that begin as indicated.

```
sage: V.i[tab key]
V.is_ambient    V.is_dense     V.is_full      V.is_sparse
```

If you wonder what a particular function does, e.g., the coordinates function, type V.coordinates? for help or V.coordinates?? for the source code, as explained in the next section.

3.8 Integrated Help System

Sage features an integrated help facility. Type a function name followed by ? for the documentation for that function.

```
sage: V = QQ^3
sage: V.coordinates?
Type:              instancemethod
Base Class:        <type 'instancemethod'>
String Form:       <bound method FreeModule_ambient_field.coordinates of Vector
space of dimension 3 over Rational Field>
Namespace:         Interactive
File:              /home/was/s/local/lib/python2.4/site-packages/sage/modules/f
ree_module.py
Definition:        V.coordinates(self, v)
Docstring:
    Write v in terms of the basis for self.

    Returns a list c such that if B is the basis for self, then
```

```
            sum c_i B_i = v.
```

If v is not in self, raises an ArithmeticError exception.

```
EXAMPLES:
    sage: M = FreeModule(IntegerRing(), 2); M0,M1=M.gens()
    sage: W = M.submodule([M0 + M1, M0 - 2*M1])
    sage: W.coordinates(2*M0-M1)
    [2, -1]
```

As shown above, the output tells you the type of the object, the file in which it is defined, and a useful description of the function with examples that you can paste into your current session. Almost all of these examples are regularly automatically tested to make sure they work and behave exactly as claimed.

Another feature that is very much in the spirit of the open source nature of Sage is that if f is a Python function, then typing f?? displays the source code that defines f. For example,

```
sage: V = QQ^3
sage: V.coordinates??
Type:           instancemethod
...
Source:
def coordinates(self, v):
    """
    Write $v$ in terms of the basis for self.
    ...
    """
    return self.coordinate_vector(v).list()
```

This tells us that all the `coordinates` function does is call the `coordinate_vector` function and change the result into a list. What does the `coordinate_vector` function do?

```
sage: V = QQ^3
sage: V.coordinate_vector??
...
def coordinate_vector(self, v):
    ...
    return self.ambient_vector_space()(v)
```

The `coordinate_vector` function coerces its input into the ambient space, which has the effect of computing the vector of coefficients of v in terms of V. The space V is already ambient since it's just $\mathbf{Q}^3$. There is also a `coordinate_vector` function for subspaces, and it's different. We create a subspace and see:

```
sage: V = QQ^3; W = V.span_of_basis([V.0, V.1])
sage: W.coordinate_vector??
...
def coordinate_vector(self, v):
    """
    ...
    """
    # First find the coordinates of v wrt echelon basis.
    w = self.echelon_coordinate_vector(v)
```

```
        # Next use transformation matrix from echelon basis to
        # user basis.
        T = self.echelon_to_user_matrix()
        return T.linear_combination_of_rows(w)
```

(If you think the implementation is inefficient, please sign up to help optimize linear algebra.)

You may also type `help(command_name)` or `help(class)` for a manpage-like help file about a given class.

```
sage: help(VectorSpace)
Help on class VectorSpace ...

class VectorSpace(__builtin__.object)
 |  Create a Vector Space.
 |
 |  To create an ambient space over a field with given dimension
 |  using the calling syntax ...
 :
 :
```

When you type q to exit the help system, your session appears just as it was. The help listing does not clutter up your session, unlike the output of `function_name?` sometimes does. It's particularly helpful to type `help(module_name)`. For example, vector spaces are defined in `sage.modules.free_module`, so type `help(sage.modules.free_module)` for documentation about that whole module. When viewing documentation using help, you can search by typing / and in reverse by typing ?.

3.9 Saving and Loading Individual Objects

Suppose you compute a matrix or worse, a complicated space of modular symbols, and would like to save it for later use. What can you do? There are several approaches that computer algebra systems take to saving individual objects.

1. **Save your Game:** Only support saving and loading of complete sessions (e.g., GAP, Magma).
2. **Unified Input/Output:** Make every object print in a way that can be read back in (GP/PARI).
3. **Eval**: Make it easy to evaluate arbitrary code in the interpreter (e.g., Singular, PARI).

Because Sage uses Python, it takes a different approach, which is that every object can be serialized, i.e., turned into a string from which that object can be recovered. This is in spirit similar to the unified I/O approach of PARI, except it doesn't have the drawback that objects print to screen in too complicated of a way. Also, support for saving and loading is (in most cases) completely automatic, requiring no extra programming; it's simply a feature of Python that was designed into the language from the ground up.

Almost all Sage objects x can be saved in compressed form to disk using `save(x, filename)` (or in many cases `x.save(filename)`). To load the object back in, use `load(filename)`.

```
sage: A = MatrixSpace(QQ,3)(range(9))^2
sage: A
[ 15  18  21]
```

```
[ 42  54  66]
[ 69  90 111]
sage: save(A, 'A')
```

You should now quit Sage and restart. Then you can get A back:

```
sage: A = load('A')
sage: A
[ 15  18  21]
[ 42  54  66]
[ 69  90 111]
```

You can do the same with more complicated objects, e.g., elliptic curves. All data about the object that is cached is stored with the object. For example,

```
sage: E = EllipticCurve('11a')
sage: v = E.anlist(100000)          # takes a while
sage: save(E, 'E')
sage: quit
```

The saved version of E takes 153 kilobytes, since it stores the first 100000 a_n with it.

```
~/tmp$ ls -l E.sobj
-rw-r--r--  1 was was 153500 2006-01-28 19:23 E.sobj
~/tmp$ sage [...]
sage: E = load('E')
sage: v = E.anlist(100000)          # instant!
```

(In Python, saving and loading is accomplished using the cPickle module. In particular, a Sage object x can be saved via cPickle.dumps(x, 2). Note the 2!)

Sage cannot save and load individual objects created in some other computer algebra systems, e.g., GAP, Singular, Maxima, etc. They reload in a state marked "invalid". In GAP, though many objects print in a form from which they can be reconstructed, many don't, so reconstructing from their print representation is purposely not allowed.

```
sage: a = gap(2)
sage: a.save('a')
sage: load('a')
Traceback (most recent call last):
...
ValueError: The session in which this object was defined is no longer
running.
```

GP/PARI objects can be saved and loaded since their print representation is enough to reconstruct them.

```
sage: a = gp(2)
sage: a.save('a')
sage: load('a')
2
```

Saved objects can be re-loaded later on computers with different architectures or operating systems, e.g., you could save a huge matrix on 32-bit OS X and reload it on 64-bit Linux, find the echelon form, then move it back. Also, in many cases you can even load objects into versions of Sage that are different than the versions they were saved in, as long as the code for that object isn't too different. All the attributes of the objects are saved, along with the class (but not source code) that defines the object. If that class no longer exists in a new version of Sage, then the object can't be reloaded in that newer version. But you could load it in an old version, get the objects dictionary (with `x.__dict__`), and save the dictionary, and load that into the newer version.

3.9.1 Saving as Text

You can also save the ASCII text representation of objects to a plain text file by simply opening a file in write mode and writing the string representation of the object (you can write many objects this way as well). When you're done writing objects, close the file.

```
sage: R.<x,y> = PolynomialRing(QQ,2)
sage: f = (x+y)^7
sage: o = open('file.txt','w')
sage: o.write(str(f))
sage: o.close()
```

3.10 Saving and Loading Complete Sessions

Sage has very flexible support for saving and loading complete sessions.

The command `save_session(sessionname)` saves all the variables you've defined in the current session as a dictionary in the given `sessionname`. (In the rare case when a variable does not support saving, it is simply not saved to the dictionary.) The resulting file is an `.sobj` file and can be loaded just like any other object that was saved. When you load the objects saved in a session, you get a dictionary whose keys are the variables names and whose values are the objects.

You can use the `load_session(sessionname)` command to load the variables defined in `sessionname` into the current session. Note that this does not wipe out variables you've already defined in your current session; instead, the two sessions are merged.

First we start Sage and define some variables.

```
sage: E = EllipticCurve('11a')
sage: M = ModularSymbols(37)
sage: a = 389
sage: t = M.T(2003).matrix(); t.charpoly().factor()
 _4 = (x - 2004) * (x - 12)^2 * (x + 54)^2
```

Next we save our session, which saves each of the above variables into a file. Then we view the file, which is about 3K in size.

```
sage: save_session('misc')
Saving a
Saving M
Saving t
Saving E
```

```
sage: quit
was@form:~/tmp$ ls -l misc.sobj
-rw-r--r-- 1 was was 2979 2006-01-28 19:47 misc.sobj
```

Finally we restart Sage, define an extra variable, and load our saved session.

```
sage: b = 19
sage: load_session('misc')
Loading a
Loading M
Loading E
Loading t
```

Each saved variable is again available. Moreover, the variable b was not overwritten.

```
sage: M
Full Modular Symbols space for Gamma_0(37) of weight 2 with sign 0
and dimension 5 over Rational Field
sage: E
Elliptic Curve defined by y^2 + y = x^3 - x^2 - 10*x - 20 over Rational
Field
sage: b
19
sage: a
389
```

3.11 The Notebook Interface

The Sage notebook is run by typing

```
sage: notebook()
```

on the command line of Sage. This starts the Sage notebook and opens your default web browser to view it. The server's state files are stored in $HOME/.sage/sage_notebook.

Other options include:

```
sage: notebook("directory")
```

which starts a new notebook server using files in the given directory, instead of the default directory $HOME/.sage/sage_notebook. This can be useful if you want to have a collection of worksheets associated with a specific project, or run several separate notebook servers at the same time.

When you start the notebook, it first creates the following files in $HOME/.sage/sage_notebook:

```
nb.sobj         (the notebook SAGE object file)
objects/        (a directory containing SAGE objects)
worksheets/     (a directory containing SAGE worksheets).
```

After creating the above files, the notebook starts a web server.

A "notebook" is a collection of user accounts, each of which can have any number of worksheets. When you create a new worksheet, the data that defines it is stored in the `worksheets/username/number` directories. In each such directory there is a plain text file `worksheet.txt` - if anything ever happens to your worksheets, or Sage, or whatever, that human-readable file contains everything needed to reconstruct your worksheet.

From within Sage, type `notebook?` for much more about how to start a notebook server.

The following diagram illustrates the architecture of the Sage Notebook:

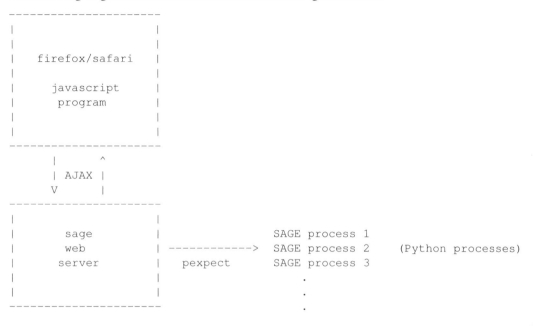

For help on a Sage command, `cmd`, in the notebook browser box, type `cmd?` and now hit `<esc>` (not `<shift-enter>`).

For help on the keyboard shortcuts available in the notebook interface, click on the `Help` link.

3.11. The Notebook Interface

CHAPTER
FOUR

INTERFACES

A central facet of Sage is that it supports computation with objects in many different computer algebra systems "under one roof" using a common interface and clean programming language.

The console and interact methods of an interface do very different things. For example, using GAP as an example:

1. `gap.console()`: This opens the GAP console - it transfers control to GAP. Here Sage is serving as nothing more than a convenient program launcher, similar to the Linux bash shell.

2. `gap.interact()`: This is a convenient way to interact with a running GAP instance that may be "full of" Sage objects. You can import Sage objects into this GAP session (even from the interactive interface), etc.

4.1 GP/PARI

PARI is a compact, very mature, highly optimized C program whose primary focus is number theory. There are two very distinct interfaces that you can use in Sage:

- `gp` - the "**G** o **P** ARI" interpreter, and
- `pari` - the PARI C library.

For example, the following are two ways of doing the same thing. They look identical, but the output is actually different, and what happens behind the scenes is drastically different.

```
sage: gp('znprimroot(10007)')
Mod(5, 10007)
sage: pari('znprimroot(10007)')
Mod(5, 10007)
```

In the first case, a separate copy of the GP interpreter is started as a server, and the string `'znprimroot(10007)'` is sent to it, evaluated by GP, and the result is assigned to a variable in GP (which takes up space in the child GP processes memory that won't be freed). Then the value of that variable is displayed. In the second case, no separate program is started, and the string `'znprimroot(10007)'` is evaluated by a certain PARI C library function. The result is stored in a piece of memory on the Python heap, which is freed when the variable is no longer referenced. The objects have different types:

```
sage: type(gp('znprimroot(10007)'))
<class 'sage.interfaces.gp.GpElement'>
sage: type(pari('znprimroot(10007)'))
<type 'sage.libs.pari.gen.gen'>
```

So which should you use? It depends on what you're doing. The GP interface can do absolutely anything you could do in the usual GP/PARI command line program, since it is running that program. In particular, you can load complicated PARI programs and run them. In contrast, the PARI interface (via the C library) is much more restrictive. First, not all member functions have been implemented. Second, a lot of code, e.g., involving numerical integration, won't work via the PARI interface. That said, the PARI interface can be significantly faster and more robust than the GP one.

(If the GP interface runs out of memory evaluating a given input line, it will silently and automatically double the stack size and retry that input line. Thus your computation won't crash if you didn't correctly anticipate the amount of memory that would be needed. This is a nice trick the usual GP interpreter doesn't seem to provide. Regarding the PARI C library interface, it immediately copies each created object off of the PARI stack, hence the stack never grows. However, each object must not exceed 100MB in size, or the stack will overflow when the object is being created. This extra copying does impose a slight performance penalty.)

In summary, Sage uses the PARI C library to provide functionality similar to that provided by the GP/PARI interpreter, except with different sophisticated memory management and the Python programming language.

First we create a PARI list from a Python list.

```
sage: v = pari([1,2,3,4,5])
sage: v
[1, 2, 3, 4, 5]
sage: type(v)
<type 'sage.libs.pari.gen.gen'>
```

Every PARI object is of type `py_pari.gen`. The PARI type of the underlying object can be obtained using the `type` member function.

```
sage: v.type()
't_VEC'
```

In PARI, to create an elliptic curve we enter `ellinit([1,2,3,4,5])`. Sage is similar, except that `ellinit` is a method that can be called on any PARI object, e.g., our `t\_VEC` v.

```
sage: e = v.ellinit()
sage: e.type()
't_VEC'
sage: pari(e)[:13]
[1, 2, 3, 4, 5, 9, 11, 29, 35, -183, -3429, -10351, 6128487/10351]
```

Now that we have an elliptic curve object, we can compute some things about it.

```
sage: e.elltors()
[1, [], []]
sage: e.ellglobalred()
[10351, [1, -1, 0, -1], 1]
sage: f = e.ellchangecurve([1,-1,0,-1])
```

```
sage: f[:5]
[1, -1, 0, 4, 3]
```

4.2 GAP

Sage comes with GAP 4.4.10 for computational discrete mathematics, especially group theory.

Here's an example of GAP's `IdGroup` function, which uses the optional small groups database that has to be installed separately, as explained below.

```
sage: G = gap('Group((1,2,3)(4,5), (3,4))')
sage: G
Group( [ (1,2,3)(4,5), (3,4) ] )
sage: G.Center()
Group( () )
sage: G.IdGroup()    # optional - database_gap
[ 120, 34 ]
sage: G.Order()
120
```

We can do the same computation in Sage without explicitly invoking the GAP interface as follows:

```
sage: G = PermutationGroup([[(1,2,3),(4,5)],[(3,4)]])
sage: G.center()
Subgroup of (Permutation Group with generators [(3,4), (1,2,3)(4,5)]) generated by [()]
sage: G.group_id()    # optional - database_gap
[120, 34]
sage: n = G.order(); n
120
```

(For some GAP functionality, you should install two optional Sage packages. Type `sage -optional` for a list and choose the one that looks like `gap\_packages-x.y.z`, then type `sage -i gap\_packages-x.y.z`. Do the same for `database\_gap-x.y.z`. Some non-GPL'd GAP packages may be installed by downloading them from the GAP web site [GAPkg], and unpacking them in `$SAGE_ROOT/local/lib/gap-4.4.10/pkg`.)

4.3 Singular

Singular provides a massive and mature library for Gröbner bases, multivariate polynomial gcds, bases of Riemann-Roch spaces of a plane curve, and factorizations, among other things. We illustrate multivariate polynomial factorization using the Sage interface to Singular (do not type the ...):

```
sage: R1 = singular.ring(0, '(x,y)', 'dp')
sage: R1
//   characteristic : 0
//   number of vars : 2
//        block   1 : ordering dp
//                  : names    x y
```

```
//            block   2 : ordering C
sage: f = singular('9*y^8 - 9*x^2*y^7 - 18*x^3*y^6 - 18*x^5*y^6 + \
...    9*x^6*y^4 + 18*x^7*y^5 + 36*x^8*y^4 + 9*x^10*y^4 - 18*x^11*y^2 - \
...    9*x^12*y^3 - 18*x^13*y^2 + 9*x^16')
```

Now that we have defined f, we print it and factor.

```
sage: f
9*x^16-18*x^13*y^2-9*x^12*y^3+9*x^10*y^4
-18*x^11*y^2+36*x^8*y^4+18*x^7*y^5
-18*x^5*y^6+9*x^6*y^4-18*x^3*y^6-9*x^2*y^7+9*y^8
sage: f.parent()
Singular
sage: F = f.factorize(); F
[1]:
   _[1]=9
   _[2]=x^6-2*x^3*y^2-x^2*y^3+y^4
   _[3]=-x^5+y^2
[2]:
   1,1,2
sage: F[1][2]
x^6-2*x^3*y^2-x^2*y^3+y^4
```

As with the GAP example in *GAP*, we can compute the above factorization without explicitly using the Singular interface (however, behind the scenes Sage uses the Singular interface for the actual computation). Do not type the ...:

```
sage: x, y = QQ['x, y'].gens()
sage: f = 9*y^8 - 9*x^2*y^7 - 18*x^3*y^6 - 18*x^5*y^6 + 9*x^6*y^4\
...      + 18*x^7*y^5 + 36*x^8*y^4 + 9*x^10*y^4 - 18*x^11*y^2 - 9*x^12*y^3\
...      - 18*x^13*y^2 + 9*x^16
sage: factor(f)
(9) * (-x^5 + y^2)^2 * (x^6 - 2*x^3*y^2 - x^2*y^3 + y^4)
```

4.4 Maxima

Maxima is included with Sage, as well as a Lisp implementation. The gnuplot package (which Maxima uses by default for plotting) is distributed as a Sage optional package. Among other things, Maxima does symbolic manipulation. Maxima can integrate and differentiate functions symbolically, solve 1st order ODEs, most linear 2nd order ODEs, and has implemented the Laplace transform method for linear ODEs of any degree. Maxima also knows about a wide range of special functions, has plotting capabilities via gnuplot, and has methods to solve and manipulate matrices (such as row reduction, eigenvalues and eigenvectors), and polynomial equations.

We illustrate the Sage/Maxima interface by constructing the matrix whose i, j entry is i/j, for $i, j = 1, \ldots, 4$.

```
sage: f = maxima.eval('ij_entry[i,j] := i/j')
sage: A = maxima('genmatrix(ij_entry,4,4)'); A
matrix([1,1/2,1/3,1/4],[2,1,2/3,1/2],[3,3/2,1,3/4],[4,2,4/3,1])
sage: A.determinant()
```

```
0
sage: A.echelon()
matrix([1,1/2,1/3,1/4],[0,0,0,0],[0,0,0,0],[0,0,0,0])
sage: A.eigenvalues()
[[0,4],[3,1]]
sage: A.eigenvectors()
[[[0,4],[3,1]],[[[1,0,0,-4],[0,1,0,-2],[0,0,1,-4/3]],[[1,2,3,4]]]]
```

Here's another example:

```
sage: A = maxima("matrix ([1, 0, 0], [1, -1, 0], [1, 3, -2])")
sage: eigA = A.eigenvectors()
sage: V = VectorSpace(QQ,3)
sage: eigA
[[[-2,-1,1],[1,1,1]],[[[0,0,1]],[[0,1,3]],[[1,1/2,5/6]]]]
sage: v1 = V(sage_eval(repr(eigA[1][0][0]))); lambda1 = eigA[0][0][0]
sage: v2 = V(sage_eval(repr(eigA[1][1][0]))); lambda2 = eigA[0][0][1]
sage: v3 = V(sage_eval(repr(eigA[1][2][0]))); lambda3 = eigA[0][0][2]

sage: M = MatrixSpace(QQ,3,3)
sage: AA = M([[1,0,0],[1, - 1,0],[1,3, - 2]])
sage: b1 = v1.base_ring()
sage: AA*v1 == b1(lambda1)*v1
True
sage: b2 = v2.base_ring()
sage: AA*v2 == b2(lambda2)*v2
True
sage: b3 = v3.base_ring()
sage: AA*v3 == b3(lambda3)*v3
True
```

Finally, we give an example of using Sage to plot using `openmath`. Many of these were modified from the Maxima reference manual.

A 2D plot of several functions (do not type the `...`):

```
sage: maxima.plot2d('[cos(7*x),cos(23*x)^4,sin(13*x)^3]','[x,0,1]',   # not tested
....:     '[plot_format,openmath]')
```

A "live" 3D plot which you can move with your mouse (do not type the `...`):

```
sage: maxima.plot3d ("2^(-u^2 + v^2)", "[u, -3, 3]", "[v, -2, 2]",   # not tested
....:     '[plot_format, openmath]')
sage: maxima.plot3d("atan(-x^2 + y^3/4)", "[x, -4, 4]", "[y, -4, 4]",   # not tested
....:     "[grid, 50, 50]",'[plot_format, openmath]')
```

The next plot is the famous Möbius strip (do not type the `...`):

```
sage: maxima.plot3d("[cos(x)*(3 + y*cos(x/2)), sin(x)*(3 + y*cos(x/2)), y*sin(x/2)]",
....:     "[x, -4, 4]", "[y, -4, 4]", '[plot_format, openmath]')
```

The next plot is the famous Klein bottle (do not type the `...`):

```
sage: maxima("expr_1: 5*cos(x)*(cos(x/2)*cos(y) + sin(x/2)*sin(2*y)+ 3.0) - 10.0")
5*cos(x)*(sin(x/2)*sin(2*y)+cos(x/2)*cos(y)+3.0)-10.0
sage: maxima("expr_2: -5*sin(x)*(cos(x/2)*cos(y) + sin(x/2)*sin(2*y)+ 3.0)")
-5*sin(x)*(sin(x/2)*sin(2*y)+cos(x/2)*cos(y)+3.0)
sage: maxima("expr_3: 5*(-sin(x/2)*cos(y) + cos(x/2)*sin(2*y))")
5*(cos(x/2)*sin(2*y)-sin(x/2)*cos(y))
sage: maxima.plot3d ("[expr_1, expr_2, expr_3]", "[x, -%pi, %pi]",    # not tested
....:      "[y, -%pi, %pi]", "['grid, 40, 40]", '[plot_format, openmath]')
```

CHAPTER
FIVE

SAGE, LATEX AND FRIENDS

AUTHOR: Rob Beezer (2010-05-23)

Sage and the LaTeX dialect of TeX have an intensely synergistic relationship. This section aims to introduce the variety of interactions, beginning with the most basic and proceeding to the more unusual and arcane. (So you may not want to read this entire section on your first pass through this tutorial.)

5.1 Overview

It may be easiest to understand the various uses of LaTeX with a brief overview of the mechanics of the three principal methods employed by Sage.

1. Every "object" in Sage is required to have a LaTeX representation. You can access this representation by executing, in the notebook or at the sage command line, `latex(foo)` where `foo` is some object in Sage. The output is a string that should render a reasonably accurate representation of `foo` when used in TeX's math-mode (for example, when enclosed between a pair of single dollar signs). Some examples of this follow below.

   In this way, Sage can be used effectively for constructing portions of a LaTeX document: create or compute an object in Sage, print `latex()` of the object and cut/paste it into your document.

2. The notebook interface is configured to use MathJax to render mathematics cleanly in a web browser. MathJax is an open source JavaScript display engine for mathematics that works in all modern browsers. It is able to render a large, but not totally complete, subset of TeX. It has no support for things like complicated tables, sectioning or document management, as it is oriented towards accurately rendering "snippets" of TeX. Seemingly automatic rendering of math in the notebook is provided by converting the `latex()` representation of an object (as described above) into a form of HTML palatable to MathJax.

   Since MathJax uses its own scalable fonts, it is superior to other methods that rely on converting equations, or other snippets of TeX, into static inline images.

3. At the Sage command-line, or in the notebook when LaTeX code is more involved than MathJax can handle, a system-wide installation of LaTeX can be employed. Sage includes almost everything you need to build and use Sage, but a significant exception is TeX itself. So in these situations you need to have TeX installed, along with some associated conversion utilities, to utilize the full power.

Here we demonstrate some basic uses of the `latex()` function.

```
sage: var('z')
z
sage: latex(z^12)
z^{12}
sage: latex(integrate(z^4, z))
\frac{1}{5} \, z^{5}
sage: latex('a string')
\text{\texttt{a{ }string}}
sage: latex(QQ)
\Bold{Q}
sage: latex(matrix(QQ, 2, 3, [[2,4,6],[-1,-1,-1]]))
\left(\begin{array}{rrr}
2 & 4 & 6 \\
-1 & -1 & -1
\end{array}\right)
```

Basic MathJax functionality is largely automatic in the notebook, but we can partially demonstrate this support with the `MathJax` class. The `eval` function of this class converts a Sage object to its LaTeX representation and then wraps it in HTML that invokes the CSS "math" class, which then employs MathJax.

```
sage: from sage.misc.latex import MathJax
sage: mj = MathJax()
sage: var('z')
z
sage: mj(z^12)
<html><...]">\newcommand{\Bold}[1]{\mathbf{#1}}z^{12}</script></html>
sage: mj(QQ)
<html><...]">\newcommand{\Bold}[1]{\mathbf{#1}}\Bold{Q}</script></html>
sage: mj(ZZ[x])
<html><...]">\newcommand{\Bold}[1]{\mathbf{#1}}\Bold{Z}[x]</script></html>
sage: mj(integrate(z^4, z))
<html><...]">\newcommand{\Bold}[1]{\mathbf{#1}}\frac{1}{5} \, z^{5}</script></html>
```

5.2 Basic Use

As indicated in the overview, the simplest way to exploit Sage's support of LaTeX is to use the `latex()` function to create legitimate LaTeX code to represent mathematical objects. These strings can then be incorporated into standalone LaTeX documents. This works identically in the notebook and at the Sage command line.

At the other extreme is the `view()` command. At the Sage command line the command `view(foo)` will create the LaTeX representation of `foo`, incorporate this into a simple LaTeX document, and then process that document with your system-wide TeX installation. Finally, the appropriate viewer will be called to display the output from the TeX command. Which version of TeX is used, and therefore the nature of the output and associated viewer, can be customized (see *Customizing LaTeX Processing*).

In the notebook, the `view(foo)` command creates the appropriate combination of HTML and CSS so that MathJax will render the LaTeX representation properly in the worksheet. To the user, it simply creates a nicely formatted version of the output, distinct from the default ASCII output of Sage. Not every mathematical object in Sage has a LaTeX representation amenable to the limited capabilities of MathJax. In these cases, the MathJax interpretation can be bypassed, the system-wide TeX called instead, and the subsequent output converted to a graphic image for display in the worksheet. Affecting and controlling this process is discussed below in the section *Customizing LaTeX Generation*.

The notebook has two other features for employing TeX. The first is the "Typeset" button just above the first cell of a worksheet, to the right of the four drop-down boxes. When checked, any subsequent evaluations of cells will result in output interpreted by MathJax, hence of a typeset quality. Note that this effect is not retroactive – previously evaluated cells need to be re-evaluated. Essentially, checking the "Typeset" button is identical to wrapping the output of each cell in the `view()` command.

A second feature of the notebook is entering TeX as part of annotating a worksheet. When the cursor is placed between cells of a worksheet so that a blue bar appears, then a shift-click will open a mini-word-processor, TinyMCE. This allows for the entry of text, using a WSIWYG editor to create HTML and CSS command for styled text. So it is possible to add formatted text as commentary within a worksheet. However, text between pairs of dollar signs, or pairs of double dollar signs is interpreted by MathJax as inline or display math (respectively).

5.3 Customizing LaTeX Generation

There are several ways to customize the actual LaTeX code generated by the `latex()` command. In the notebook and at the Sage command-line there is a pre-defined object named `latex` which has several methods, which you can list by typing `latex.`, followed by the tab key (note the period).

A good example is the `latex.matrix_delimiters` method. It can be used to change the notation surrounding a matrix – large parentheses, brackets, braces, vertical bars. No notion of style is enforced, you can mix and match as you please. Notice how the backslashes needed in LaTeX require an extra slash so they are escaped properly within the Python string.

```
sage: A = matrix(ZZ, 2, 2, range(4))
sage: latex(A)
\left(\begin{array}{rr}
0 & 1 \\
2 & 3
\end{array}\right)
sage: latex.matrix_delimiters(left='[', right=']')
sage: latex(A)
\left[\begin{array}{rr}
0 & 1 \\
2 & 3
\end{array}\right]
sage: latex.matrix_delimiters(left='\\{', right='\\}')
sage: latex(A)
\left\{\begin{array}{rr}
0 & 1 \\
2 & 3
\end{array}\right\}
```

The `latex.vector_delimiters` method works similarly.

The way common rings and fields (integers, rational, reals, etc.) are typeset can be controlled by the
`latex.blackboard_bold` method. These sets are by default typeset in bold, but may optionally be
written in a double-struck fashion as sometimes done in written work. This is accomplished by redefining the
`\Bold{}` macro which is built-in to Sage.

```
sage: latex(QQ)
\Bold{Q}
sage: from sage.misc.latex import MathJax
sage: mj=MathJax()
sage: mj(QQ)
<html><[...]">\newcommand{\Bold}[1]{\mathbf{#1}}\Bold{Q}</script></html>
sage: latex.blackboard_bold(True)
sage: mj(QQ)
<html><[...]">\newcommand{\Bold}[1]{\mathbb{#1}}\Bold{Q}</script></html>
sage: latex.blackboard_bold(False)
```

It is possible to take advantage of the extensible nature of TeX by adding in new macros and new packages.
First, individual macros can be added so that they are used when MathJax interprets a snippet of TeX in the
notebook.

```
sage: latex.extra_macros()
''
sage: latex.add_macro("\\newcommand{\\foo}{bar}")
sage: latex.extra_macros()
'\\newcommand{\\foo}{bar}'
sage: var('x y')
(x, y)
sage: latex(x+y)
x + y
sage: from sage.misc.latex import MathJax
sage: mj=MathJax()
sage: mj(x+y)
<html><[...]">\n[...]{\Bold}[1]{\mathbf{#1}}\n[...]{\foo}{bar}x + y</script></html>
```

Additional macros added this way will also be used in the event that the system-wide version of TeX is called
on something larger than MathJax can handle. The command `latex_extra_preamble` is used to build
the preamble of a complete LaTeX document, so the following illustrates how this is accomplished. As usual
note the need for the double-backslashes in the Python strings.

```
sage: latex.extra_macros('')
sage: latex.extra_preamble('')
sage: from sage.misc.latex import latex_extra_preamble
sage: print latex_extra_preamble()
\newcommand{\ZZ}{\Bold{Z}}
...
\newcommand{\Bold}[1]{\mathbf{#1}}
sage: latex.add_macro("\\newcommand{\\foo}{bar}")
sage: print latex_extra_preamble()
\newcommand{\ZZ}{\Bold{Z}}
...
\newcommand{\Bold}[1]{\mathbf{#1}}
\newcommand{\foo}{bar}
```

Again, for larger or more complicated LaTeX expressions, it is possible to add packages (or anything else) to the preamble of the LaTeX file. Anything may be incorporated into the preamble with the `latex.add_to_preamble` command, and the specialized command `latex.add_package_to_preamble_if_available` will first check if a certain package is actually available before trying to add it to the preamble.

Here we add the geometry package to the preamble and use it to set the size of the region on the page that TeX will use (effectively setting the margins). As usual, note the need for the double-backslashes in the Python strings.

```
sage: from sage.misc.latex import latex_extra_preamble
sage: latex.extra_macros('')
sage: latex.extra_preamble('')
sage: latex.add_to_preamble('\\usepackage{geometry}')
sage: latex.add_to_preamble('\\geometry{letterpaper,total={8in,10in}}')
sage: latex.extra_preamble()
'\\usepackage{geometry}\\geometry{letterpaper,total={8in,10in}}'
sage: print latex_extra_preamble()
\usepackage{geometry}\geometry{letterpaper,total={8in,10in}}
\newcommand{\ZZ}{\Bold{Z}}
...
\newcommand{\Bold}[1]{\mathbf{#1}}
```

A particular package may be added along with a check on its existence, as follows. As an example, we just illustrate an attempt to add to the preamble a package that presumably does not exist.

```
sage: latex.extra_preamble('')
sage: latex.extra_preamble()
''
sage: latex.add_to_preamble('\\usepackage{foo-bar-unchecked}')
sage: latex.extra_preamble()
'\\usepackage{foo-bar-unchecked}'
sage: latex.add_package_to_preamble_if_available('foo-bar-checked')
sage: latex.extra_preamble()
'\\usepackage{foo-bar-unchecked}'
```

5.4 Customizing LaTeX Processing

It is also possible to control which variant of TeX is used for system-wide invocations, thus also influencing the nature of the output. Similarly, it is also possible to control when the notebook will use MathJax (simple TeX snippets) or the system-wide TeX installation (more complicated LaTeX expressions).

The `latex.engine()` command can be used to control if the system-wide executables `latex`, `pdflatex` or `xelatex` are employed for more complicated LaTeX expressions. When `view()` is called from the sage command-line and the engine is set to `latex`, a dvi file is produced and Sage will use a dvi viewer (like xdvi) to display the result. In contrast, using `view()` at the Sage command-line, when the engine is set to `pdflatex`, will produce a PDF as the result and Sage will call your system's utility for displaying PDF files (acrobat, okular, evince, etc.).

In the notebook, it is necessary to intervene in the decision as to whether MathJax will interpret a snippet of TeX, or if the LaTeX is complicated enough that the system-wide installation of TeX should do the work instead. The device is a list of strings, which if any one is discovered in a piece of LaTeX code signal the notebook to bypass MathJax and invoke latex (or whichever executable is set by the `latex.engine()` command). This list is managed by the `latex.add_to_mathjax_avoid_list` and `latex.mathjax_avoid_list` commands.

```
sage: latex.mathjax_avoid_list([])
sage: latex.mathjax_avoid_list()
[]
sage: latex.mathjax_avoid_list(['foo', 'bar'])
sage: latex.mathjax_avoid_list()
['foo', 'bar']
sage: latex.add_to_mathjax_avoid_list('tikzpicture')
sage: latex.mathjax_avoid_list()
['foo', 'bar', 'tikzpicture']
sage: latex.mathjax_avoid_list([])
sage: latex.mathjax_avoid_list()
[]
```

Suppose a LaTeX expression is produced in the notebook with `view()` or while the "Typeset" button is checked, and then recognized as requiring the external LaTeX installation through the "mathjax avoid list." Then the selected executable (as specified by `latex.engine()`) will process the LaTeX. However, instead of then spawning an external viewer (which is the command-line behavior), Sage will attempt to convert the result into a single, tightly-cropped image, which is then inserted into the worksheet as the output of the cell.

Just how this conversion proceeds depends on several factors – mostly which executable you have specified as the engine and which conversion utilities are available on your system. Four useful converters that will cover all eventualities are `dvips`, `ps2pdf`, `dvipng` and from the `ImageMagick` suite, `convert`. The goal is to produce a PNG file as the output for inclusion back into the worksheet. When a LaTeX expression can be converted successfully to a dvi by the latex engine, then dvipng should accomplish the conversion. If the LaTeX expression and chosen engine creates a dvi with specials that dvipng cannot handle, then dvips will create a PostScript file. Such a PostScript file, or a PDF file created by an engine such as `pdflatex`, is then processed into a PNG with the `convert` utility. The presence of two of these converters can be tested with the `have_dvipng()` and `have_convert()` routines.

These conversions are done automatically if you have the necessary converters installed; if not, then an error message is printed telling you what's missing and where to download it.

For a concrete example of how complicated LaTeX expressions can be processed, see the example in the next section (*An Example: Combinatorial Graphs with tkz-graph*) for using the LaTeX `tkz-graph` package to produce high-quality renderings of combinatorial graphs. For other examples, there are some pre-packaged test cases. To use these, it is necessary to import the `sage.misc.latex.latex_examples` object, which is an instance of the `sage.misc.latex.LatexExamples` class, as illustrated below. This class currently has examples of commutative diagrams, combinatorial graphs, knot theory and pstricks, which respectively exercise the following packages: xy, tkz-graph, xypic, pstricks. After the import, use tab-completion on `latex_examples` to see the pre-packaged examples. Calling each example will give you back some explanation about what is required to make the example render properly. To actually see the examples, it is necessary to use `view()` (once the preamble, engine, etc are all set properly).

```
sage: from sage.misc.latex import latex_examples
sage: latex_examples.diagram()
LaTeX example for testing display of a commutative diagram produced
by xypic.

To use, try to view this object -- it won't work.  Now try
'latex.add_to_preamble("\\usepackage[matrix,arrow,curve,cmtip]{xy}")',
and try viewing again -- it should work in the command line but not
from the notebook.  In the notebook, run
'latex.add_to_mathjax_avoid_list("xymatrix")' and try again -- you
should get a picture (a part of the diagram arising from a filtered
chain complex).
```

5.5 An Example: Combinatorial Graphs with tkz-graph

High-quality illustrations of combinatorial graphs (henceforth just "graphs") are possible with the `tkz-graph` package. This package is built on top of the `tikz` front-end to the `pgf` library. So all of these components need to be part of a system-wide TeX installation, and it may be possible that these components may not be at their most current versions as packaged in some TeX implementations. So for best results, it could be necessary or advisable to install these as part of your personal texmf tree. Creating, maintaining and customizing a system-wide or personal TeX installation is beyond the scope of this document, but it should be easy to find instructions. The necessary files are listed in *A Fully Capable TeX Installation*.

Thus, to start we need to insure that the relevant packages are included by adding them to the preamble of the eventual LaTeX document. The images of graphs do not form properly when a dvi file is used as an intermediate format, so it is best to set the latex engine to the `pdflatex` executable. At this point a command like `view(graphs.CompleteGraph(4))` should succeed at the Sage command-line and produce a PDF with an appropriate image of the complete graph K_4.

For a similar experience in the notebook, it is necessary to disable MathJax processing of the LaTeX code for the graph by using the "mathjax avoid list." Graphs are included with a `tikzpicture` environment, so this is a good choice for a string to include in the avoidance list. Now, `view(graphs.CompleteGraph(4))` in a worksheet should call pdflatex to create a PDF and then the `convert` utility will extract a PNG graphic to insert into the output cell of the worksheet. The following commands illustrate the steps to get graphs processed by LaTeX in the notebook.

```
sage: from sage.graphs.graph_latex import setup_latex_preamble
sage: setup_latex_preamble()
sage: latex.extra_preamble()    # random - depends on system's TeX installation
'\\usepackage{tikz}\n\\usepackage{tkz-graph}\n\\usepackage{tkz-berge}\n'
sage: latex.engine('pdflatex')
sage: latex.add_to_mathjax_avoid_list('tikzpicture')
sage: latex.mathjax_avoid_list()
['tikzpicture']
```

At this point, a command like `view(graphs.CompleteGraph(4))` should produce a graphic version of the graph pasted into the notebook, having used `pdflatex` to process `tkz-graph` commands to realize the graph. Note that there is a variety of options to affect how a graph is rendered in LaTeX via `tkz-graph`, which is again outside the scope of this section, see the section of the Reference manual titled "LaTeX Options for Graphs" for instructions and details.

5.6 A Fully Capable TeX Installation

Many of the more advanced features of the integration of TeX with Sage requires a system-wide installation of TeX. Many versions of Linux have base TeX packages based on TeX-live, for OSX there is TeXshop and for Windows there is MikTeX. The `convert` utility is part of the ImageMagick suite (which should be a package or an easy download), and the three programs `dvipng`, `ps2pdf`, and `dvips` may be included with your TeX distribution. The first two may also be obtained, respectively, from http://sourceforge.net/projects/dvipng/ and as part of Ghostscript.

Rendering combinatorial graphs requires a recent version of the PGF library, and the files `tkz-graph.sty`, `tkz-arith.sty` and perhaps `tkz-berge.sty`, all from the Altermundus site.

5.7 External Programs

There are three programs available to further integrate TeX and Sage. The first is sagetex. A concise description of sagetex is that it is a collection of TeX macros that allow a LaTeX document to include instructions to have Sage compute various objects and/or format objects using the `latex()` support built in to Sage. So as an intermediate step of compiling a LaTeX document, all of the computational and LaTeX-formatting features of Sage can be handled automatically. As an example, a mathematics examination can maintain a correct correspondence between questions and answers by using sagetex to have Sage compute one from the other. See *Using SageTeX* for more information.

tex2sws begins with a LaTeX document, but defines extra environments for the placement of Sage code. When processed with the right tools, the result is a Sage worksheet, with content properly formatted for MathJax and the Sage code incorporated as input cells. So a textbook or article can be authored in LaTeX, blocks of Sage code included, and the whole document can be transformed into a Sage worksheet where the mathematical text is nicely formatted and the blocks of Sage code are "live." Currently in development, see tex2sws @ BitBucket for more information.

sws2tex reverses the process by beginning with a Sage worksheet and converting it to legitimate LaTeX for subsequent processing with all the tools available for LaTeX documents. Currently in development, see sws2tex @ BitBucket for more information.

CHAPTER SIX

PROGRAMMING

6.1 Loading and Attaching Sage files

Next we illustrate how to load programs written in a separate file into Sage. Create a file called `example.sage` with the following content:

```
print "Hello World"
print 2^3
```

You can read in and execute `example.sage` file using the `load` command.

```
sage: load "example.sage"
Hello World
8
```

You can also attach a Sage file to a running session using the `attach` command:

```
sage: attach "example.sage"
Hello World
8
```

Now if you change `example.sage` and enter one blank line into Sage (i.e., hit `return`), then the contents of `example.sage` will be automatically reloaded into Sage.

In particular, `attach` automatically reloads a file whenever it changes, which is handy when debugging code, whereas `load` only loads a file once.

When Sage loads `example.sage` it converts it to Python, which is then executed by the Python interpreter. This conversion is minimal; it mainly involves wrapping integer literals in `Integer()` floating point literals in `RealNumber()`, replacing `^`'s by `**`'s, and replacing e.g., `R.2` by `R.gen(2)`. The converted version of `example.sage` is contained in the same directory as `example.sage` and is called `example.sage.py`. This file contains the following code:

```
print "Hello World"
print Integer(2)**Integer(3)
```

Integer literals are wrapped and the `^` is replaced by a `**`. (In Python `^` means "exclusive or" and `**` means "exponentiation".)

This preparsing is implemented in `sage/misc/interpreter.py`.)

You can paste multi-line indented code into Sage as long as there are newlines to make new blocks (this is not necessary in files). However, the best way to enter such code into Sage is to save it to a file and use `attach`, as described above.

6.2 Creating Compiled Code

Speed is crucial in mathematical computations. Though Python is a convenient very high-level language, certain calculations can be several orders of magnitude faster than in Python if they are implemented using static types in a compiled language. Some aspects of Sage would have been too slow if it had been written entirely in Python. To deal with this, Sage supports a compiled "version" of Python called Cython ([Cyt] and [Pyr]). Cython is simultaneously similar to both Python and C. Most Python constructions, including list comprehensions, conditional expressions, code like += are allowed; you can also import code that you have written in other Python modules. Moreover, you can declare arbitrary C variables, and arbitrary C library calls can be made directly. The resulting code is converted to C and compiled using a C compiler.

In order to make your own compiled Sage code, give the file an `.spyx` extension (instead of `.sage`). If you are working with the command-line interface, you can attach and load compiled code exactly like with interpreted code (at the moment, attaching and loading Cython code is not supported with the notebook interface). The actual compilation is done "behind the scenes" without your having to do anything explicit. See `$SAGE_ROOT/examples/programming/sagex/factorial.spyx` for an example of a compiled implementation of the factorial function that directly uses the GMP C library. To try this out for yourself, cd to `$SAGE_ROOT/examples/programming/sagex/`, then do the following:

```
sage: load "factorial.spyx"
***************************************************
                Recompiling factorial.spyx
***************************************************
sage: factorial(50)
30414093201713378043612608166064768844377641568960512000000000000L
sage: time n = factorial(10000)
CPU times: user 0.03 s, sys: 0.00 s, total: 0.03 s
Wall time: 0.03
```

Here the trailing L indicates a Python long integer (see *The Pre-Parser: Differences between Sage and Python*).

Note that Sage will recompile `factorial.spyx` if you quit and restart Sage. The compiled shared object library is stored under `$HOME/.sage/temp/hostname/pid/spyx`. These files are deleted when you exit Sage.

NO Sage preparsing is applied to spyx files, e.g., `1/3` will result in 0 in a spyx file instead of the rational number 1/3. If `foo` is a function in the Sage library, to use it from a spyx file import `sage.all` and use `sage.all.foo`.

```
import sage.all
def foo(n):
    return sage.all.factorial(n)
```

6.2.1 Accessing C Functions in Separate Files

It is also easy to access C functions defined in separate *.c files. Here's an example. Create files `test.c` and `test.spyx` in the same directory with contents:

The pure C code: `test.c`

```
int add_one(int n) {
  return n + 1;
}
```

The Cython code: `test.spyx`:

```
cdef extern from "test.c":
    int add_one(int n)

def test(n):
    return add_one(n)
```

Then the following works:

```
sage: attach "test.spyx"
Compiling (...)/test.spyx...
sage: test(10)
11
```

If an additional library `foo` is needed to compile the C code generated from a Cython file, add the line `clib foo` to the Cython source. Similarly, an additional C file `bar` can be included in the compilation with the declaration `cfile bar`.

6.3 Standalone Python/Sage Scripts

The following standalone Sage script factors integers, polynomials, etc:

```
#!/usr/bin/env sage -python

import sys
from sage.all import *

if len(sys.argv) != 2:
    print "Usage: %s <n>"%sys.argv[0]
    print "Outputs the prime factorization of n."
    sys.exit(1)

print factor(sage_eval(sys.argv[1]))
```

In order to use this script, your `SAGE_ROOT` must be in your PATH. If the above script is called `factor`, here is an example usage:

```
bash $ ./factor 2006
2 * 17 * 59
```

```
bash $ ./factor "32*x^5-1"
(2*x - 1) * (16*x^4 + 8*x^3 + 4*x^2 + 2*x + 1)
```

6.4 Data Types

Every object in Sage has a well-defined type. Python has a wide range of basic built-in types, and the Sage library adds many more. Some built-in Python types include strings, lists, tuples, ints and floats, as illustrated:

```
sage: s = "sage"; type(s)
<type 'str'>
sage: s = 'sage'; type(s)          # you can use either single or double quotes
<type 'str'>
sage: s = [1,2,3,4]; type(s)
<type 'list'>
sage: s = (1,2,3,4); type(s)
<type 'tuple'>
sage: s = int(2006); type(s)
<type 'int'>
sage: s = float(2006); type(s)
<type 'float'>
```

To this, Sage adds many other types. E.g., vector spaces:

```
sage: V = VectorSpace(QQ, 1000000); V
Vector space of dimension 1000000 over Rational Field
sage: type(V)
<class 'sage.modules.free_module.FreeModule_ambient_field_with_category'>
```

Only certain functions can be called on V. In other math software systems, these would be called using the "functional" notation foo(V,...). In Sage, certain functions are attached to the type (or class) of V, and are called using an object-oriented syntax like in Java or C++, e.g., V.foo(...). This helps keep the global namespace from being polluted with tens of thousands of functions, and means that many different functions with different behavior can be named foo, without having to use type-checking of arguments (or case statements) to decide which to call. Also, if you reuse the name of a function, that function is still available (e.g., if you call something zeta, then want to compute the value of the Riemann-Zeta function at 0.5, you can still type s=.5; s.zeta()).

```
sage: zeta = -1
sage: s=.5; s.zeta()
-1.46035450880959
```

In some very common cases, the usual functional notation is also supported for convenience and because mathematical expressions might look confusing using object-oriented notation. Here are some examples.

```
sage: n = 2; n.sqrt()
sqrt(2)
sage: sqrt(2)
sqrt(2)
sage: V = VectorSpace(QQ,2)
sage: V.basis()
```

```
    [
    (1, 0),
    (0, 1)
    ]
sage: basis(V)
    [
    (1, 0),
    (0, 1)
    ]
sage: M = MatrixSpace(GF(7), 2); M
Full MatrixSpace of 2 by 2 dense matrices over Finite Field of size 7
sage: A = M([1,2,3,4]); A
[1 2]
[3 4]
sage: A.charpoly('x')
x^2 + 2*x + 5
sage: charpoly(A, 'x')
x^2 + 2*x + 5
```

To list all member functions for A, use tab completion. Just type A., then type the [tab] key on your keyboard, as explained in *Reverse Search and Tab Completion*.

6.5 Lists, Tuples, and Sequences

The list data type stores elements of arbitrary type. Like in C, C++, etc. (but unlike most standard computer algebra systems), the elements of the list are indexed starting from 0:

```
sage: v = [2, 3, 5, 'x', SymmetricGroup(3)]; v
[2, 3, 5, 'x', Symmetric group of order 3! as a permutation group]
sage: type(v)
<type 'list'>
sage: v[0]
2
sage: v[2]
5
```

(When indexing into a list, it is OK if the index is not a Python int!) A Sage Integer (or Rational, or anything with an __index__ method) will work just fine.

```
sage: v = [1,2,3]
sage: v[2]
3
sage: n = 2        # SAGE Integer
sage: v[n]         # Perfectly OK!
3
sage: v[int(n)]    # Also OK.
3
```

The range function creates a list of Python int's (not Sage Integers):

```
sage: range(1, 15)
[1, 2, 3, 4, 5, 6, 7, 8, 9, 10, 11, 12, 13, 14]
```

This is useful when using list comprehensions to construct lists:

```
sage: L = [factor(n) for n in range(1, 15)]
sage: print L
[1, 2, 3, 2^2, 5, 2 * 3, 7, 2^3, 3^2, 2 * 5, 11, 2^2 * 3, 13, 2 * 7]
sage: L[12]
13
sage: type(L[12])
<class 'sage.structure.factorization_integer.IntegerFactorization'>
sage: [factor(n) for n in range(1, 15) if is_odd(n)]
[1, 3, 5, 7, 3^2, 11, 13]
```

For more about how to create lists using list comprehensions, see [PyT].

List slicing is a wonderful feature. If L is a list, then L[m:n] returns the sublist of L obtained by starting at the mth element and stopping at the $(n-1)^{st}$ element, as illustrated below.

```
sage: L = [factor(n) for n in range(1, 20)]
sage: L[4:9]
[5, 2 * 3, 7, 2^3, 3^2]
sage: print L[:4]
[1, 2, 3, 2^2]
sage: L[14:4]
[]
sage: L[14:]
[3 * 5, 2^4, 17, 2 * 3^2, 19]
```

Tuples are similar to lists, except they are immutable, meaning once they are created they can't be changed.

```
sage: v = (1,2,3,4); v
(1, 2, 3, 4)
sage: type(v)
<type 'tuple'>
sage: v[1] = 5
Traceback (most recent call last):
...
TypeError: 'tuple' object does not support item assignment
```

Sequences are a third list-oriented Sage type. Unlike lists and tuples, Sequence is not a built-in Python type. By default, a sequence is mutable, but using the Sequence class method set_immutable, it can be set to be immutable, as the following example illustrates. All elements of a sequence have a common parent, called the sequences universe.

```
sage: v = Sequence([1,2,3,4/5])
sage: v
[1, 2, 3, 4/5]
sage: type(v)
<class 'sage.structure.sequence.Sequence_generic'>
sage: type(v[1])
<type 'sage.rings.rational.Rational'>
```

```
sage: v.universe()
Rational Field
sage: v.is_immutable()
False
sage: v.set_immutable()
sage: v[0] = 3
Traceback (most recent call last):
...
ValueError: object is immutable; please change a copy instead.
```

Sequences derive from lists and can be used anywhere a list can be used:

```
sage: v = Sequence([1,2,3,4/5])
sage: isinstance(v, list)
True
sage: list(v)
[1, 2, 3, 4/5]
sage: type(list(v))
<type 'list'>
```

As another example, basis for vector spaces are immutable sequences, since it's important that you don't change them.

```
sage: V = QQ^3; B = V.basis(); B
[
(1, 0, 0),
(0, 1, 0),
(0, 0, 1)
]
sage: type(B)
<class 'sage.structure.sequence.Sequence_generic'>
sage: B[0] = B[1]
Traceback (most recent call last):
...
ValueError: object is immutable; please change a copy instead.
sage: B.universe()
Vector space of dimension 3 over Rational Field
```

6.6 Dictionaries

A dictionary (also sometimes called an associative array) is a mapping from 'hashable' objects (e.g., strings, numbers, and tuples of such; see the Python documentation http://docs.python.org/tut/node7.html and http://docs.python.org/lib/typesmapping.html for details) to arbitrary objects.

```
sage: d = {1:5, 'sage':17, ZZ:GF(7)}
sage: type(d)
<type 'dict'>
sage: d.keys()
[1, 'sage', Integer Ring]
sage: d['sage']
```

```
17
sage: d[ZZ]
Finite Field of size 7
sage: d[1]
5
```

The third key illustrates that the indexes of a dictionary can be complicated, e.g., the ring of integers.

You can turn the above dictionary into a list with the same data:

```
sage: d.items()
[(1, 5), ('sage', 17), (Integer Ring, Finite Field of size 7)]
```

A common idiom is to iterate through the pairs in a dictionary:

```
sage: d = {2:4, 3:9, 4:16}
sage: [a*b for a, b in d.iteritems()]
[8, 27, 64]
```

A dictionary is unordered, as the last output illustrates.

6.7 Sets

Python has a built-in set type. The main feature it offers is very fast lookup of whether an element is in the set or not, along with standard set-theoretic operations.

```
sage: X = set([1,19,'a']);   Y = set([1,1,1, 2/3])
sage: X
set(['a', 1, 19])
sage: Y
set([1, 2/3])
sage: 'a' in X
True
sage: 'a' in Y
False
sage: X.intersection(Y)
set([1])
```

Sage also has its own set type that is (in some cases) implemented using the built-in Python set type, but has a little bit of extra Sage-related functionality. Create a Sage set using Set(...). For example,

```
sage: X = Set([1,19,'a']);   Y = Set([1,1,1, 2/3])
sage: X
{'a', 1, 19}
sage: Y
{1, 2/3}
sage: X.intersection(Y)
{1}
sage: print latex(Y)
\left\{1, \frac{2}{3}\right\}
```

```
sage: Set(ZZ)
Set of elements of Integer Ring
```

6.8 Iterators

Iterators are a recent addition to Python that are particularly useful in mathematics applications. Here are several examples; see [PyT] for more details. We make an iterator over the squares of the nonnegative integers up to 10000000.

```
sage: v = (n^2 for n in xrange(10000000))
sage: v.next()
0
sage: v.next()
1
sage: v.next()
4
```

We create an iterate over the primes of the form $4p + 1$ with p also prime, and look at the first few values.

```
sage: w = (4*p + 1 for p in Primes() if is_prime(4*p+1))
sage: w          # in the next line, 0xb0853d6c is a random 0x number
<generator object at 0xb0853d6c>
sage: w.next()
13
sage: w.next()
29
sage: w.next()
53
```

Certain rings, e.g., finite fields and the integers have iterators associated to them:

```
sage: [x for x in GF(7)]
[0, 1, 2, 3, 4, 5, 6]
sage: W = ((x,y) for x in ZZ for y in ZZ)
sage: W.next()
(0, 0)
sage: W.next()
(0, 1)
sage: W.next()
(0, -1)
```

6.9 Loops, Functions, Control Statements, and Comparisons

We have seen a few examples already of some common uses of `for` loops. In Python, a `for` loop has an indented structure, such as

```
>>> for i in range(5):
...     print(i)
...
0
1
2
3
4
```

Note the colon at the end of the for statement (there is no "do" or "od" as in GAP or Maple), and the indentation before the "body" of the loop, namely `print(i)`. This indentation is important. In Sage, the indentation is automatically put in for you when you hit enter after a ":", as illustrated below.

```
sage: for i in range(5):
....:     print(i)   # now hit enter twice
....:
0
1
2
3
4
```

The symbol = is used for assignment. The symbol == is used to check for equality:

```
sage: for i in range(15):
....:     if gcd(i,15) == 1:
....:         print(i)
....:
1
2
4
7
8
11
13
14
```

Keep in mind how indentation determines the block structure for `if`, `for`, and `while` statements:

```
sage: def legendre(a,p):
...       is_sqr_modp=-1
...       for i in range(p):
...           if a % p == i^2 % p:
...               is_sqr_modp=1
...       return is_sqr_modp

sage: legendre(2,7)
1
sage: legendre(3,7)
-1
```

Of course this is not an efficient implementation of the Legendre symbol! It is meant to illustrate various aspects of Python/Sage programming. The function {kronecker}, which comes with Sage, computes the

Legendre symbol efficiently via a C-library call to PARI.

Finally, we note that comparisons, such as ==, !=, <=, >=, >, <, between numbers will automatically convert both numbers into the same type if possible:

```
sage: 2 < 3.1; 3.1 <= 1
True
False
sage: 2/3 < 3/2;   3/2 < 3/1
True
True
```

Almost any two objects may be compared; there is no assumption that the objects are equipped with a total ordering.

```
sage: 2 < CC(3.1,1)
True
sage: 5 < VectorSpace(QQ,3)    # output can be somewhat random
True
```

Use bool for symbolic inequalities:

```
sage: x < x + 1
x < x + 1
sage: bool(x < x + 1)
True
```

When comparing objects of different types in Sage, in most cases Sage tries to find a canonical coercion of both objects to a common parent (see *Parents, Conversion and Coercion* for more details). If successful, the comparison is performed between the coerced objects; if not successful, the objects are considered not equal. For testing whether two variables reference the same object use is. As we see in this example, the Python int 1 is unique, but the Sage Integer 1 is not:

```
sage: 1 is 2/2
False
sage: int(1) is int(2)/int(2)
True
sage: 1 is 1
False
sage: 1 == 2/2
True
```

In the following two lines, the first equality is False because there is no canonical morphism $\mathbf{Q} \to \mathbf{F}_5$, hence no canonical way to compare the 1 in $\mathbf{F}_5$ to the $1 \in \mathbf{Q}$. In contrast, there is a canonical map $\mathbf{Z} \to \mathbf{F}_5$, hence the second comparison is True. Note also that the order doesn't matter.

```
sage: GF(5)(1) == QQ(1); QQ(1) == GF(5)(1)
False
False
sage: GF(5)(1) == ZZ(1); ZZ(1) == GF(5)(1)
True
True
sage: ZZ(1) == QQ(1)
True
```

WARNING: Comparison in Sage is more restrictive than in Magma, which declares the $1 \in \mathbf{F}_5$ equal to $1 \in \mathbf{Q}$.

```
sage: magma('GF(5)!1 eq Rationals()!1')       # optional - magma
true
```

6.10 Profiling

Section Author: Martin Albrecht (malb@informatik.uni-bremen.de)

> "Premature optimization is the root of all evil." - Donald Knuth

Sometimes it is useful to check for bottlenecks in code to understand which parts take the most computational time; this can give a good idea of which parts to optimize. Python and therefore Sage offers several profiling–as this process is called–options.

The simplest to use is the `prun` command in the interactive shell. It returns a summary describing which functions took how much computational time. To profile (the currently slow! - as of version 1.0) matrix multiplication over finite fields, for example, do:

```
sage: k,a = GF(2**8,'a').objgen()
sage: A = Matrix(k,10,10,[k.random_element() for _ in range(10*10)])

sage: %prun B = A*A
       32893 function calls in 1.100 CPU seconds

Ordered by: internal time

ncalls tottime percall cumtime percall filename:lineno(function)
 12127   0.160   0.000   0.160   0.000 :0(isinstance)
  2000   0.150   0.000   0.280   0.000 matrix.py:2235(__getitem__)
  1000   0.120   0.000   0.370   0.000 finite_field_element.py:392(__mul__)
  1903   0.120   0.000   0.200   0.000 finite_field_element.py:47(__init__)
  1900   0.090   0.000   0.220   0.000 finite_field_element.py:376(__compat)
   900   0.080   0.000   0.260   0.000 finite_field_element.py:380(__add__)
     1   0.070   0.070   1.100   1.100 matrix.py:864(__mul__)
  2105   0.070   0.000   0.070   0.000 matrix.py:282(ncols)
   ...
```

Here `ncalls` is the number of calls, `tottime` is the total time spent in the given function (and excluding time made in calls to sub-functions), `percall` is the quotient of `tottime` divided by `ncalls`. `cumtime` is the total time spent in this and all sub-functions (i.e., from invocation until exit), `percall` is the quotient of `cumtime` divided by primitive calls, and `filename:lineno(function)` provides the respective data of each function. The rule of thumb here is: The higher the function in that listing, the more expensive it is. Thus it is more interesting for optimization.

As usual, `prun?` provides details on how to use the profiler and understand the output.

The profiling data may be written to an object as well to allow closer examination:

```
sage: %prun -r A*A
sage: stats = _
sage: stats?
```

Note: entering `stats = prun -r A\*A` displays a syntax error message because prun is an IPython shell command, not a regular function.

For a nice graphical representation of profiling data, you can use the hotshot profiler, a small script called `hotshot2cachetree` and the program `kcachegrind` (Unix only). The same example with the hotshot profiler:

```
sage: k,a = GF(2**8, 'a').objgen()
sage: A = Matrix(k,10,10,[k.random_element() for _ in range(10*10)])
sage: import hotshot
sage: filename = "pythongrind.prof"
sage: prof = hotshot.Profile(filename, lineevents=1)

sage: prof.run("A*A")
<hotshot.Profile instance at 0x414c11ec>
sage: prof.close()
```

This results in a file `pythongrind.prof` in the current working directory. It can now be converted to the cachegrind format for visualization.

On a system shell, type

```
hotshot2calltree -o cachegrind.out.42 pythongrind.prof
```

The output file `cachegrind.out.42` can now be examined with `kcachegrind`. Please note that the naming convention `cachegrind.out.XX` needs to be obeyed.

CHAPTER
SEVEN

USING SAGETEX

The SageTeX package allows you to embed the results of Sage computations into a LaTeX document. It comes standard with Sage. To use it, you will need to "install" it into your local TeX system; here "install" means copying a single file. See *Installation* in this tutorial and the "Make SageTeX known to TeX" section of the Sage installation guide (this link should take you to a local copy of the installation guide) for more information on doing that.

Here is a very brief example of using SageTeX. The full documentation can be found in SAGE_ROOT/local/share/texmf/tex/generic/sagetex, where SAGE_ROOT is the directory where your Sage installation is located. That directory contains the documentation, an example file, and some possibly useful Python scripts.

To see how SageTeX works, follow the directions for installing SageTeX (in *Installation*) and copy the following text into a file named, say, st_example.tex:

> **Warning:** The text below will have several errors about unknown control sequences if you are viewing this in the "live" help. Use the static version to see the correct text.

```
\documentclass{article}
\usepackage{sagetex}

\begin{document}

Using Sage\TeX, one can use Sage to compute things and put them into
your \LaTeX{} document. For example, there are
$\sage{number_of_partitions(1269)}$ integer partitions of $1269$.
You don't need to compute the number yourself, or even cut and paste
it from somewhere.

Here's some Sage code:

\begin{sageblock}
    f(x) = exp(x) * sin(2*x)
\end{sageblock}

The second derivative of $f$ is
```

99

```
\[
  \frac{\mathrm{d}^{2}}{\mathrm{d}x^{2}} \sage{f(x)} =
  \sage{diff(f, x, 2)(x)}.
\]

Here's a plot of $f$ from $-1$ to $1$:

\sageplot{plot(f, -1, 1)}

\end{document}
```

Run LaTeX on `st_example.tex` as usual. Note that LaTeX will have some complaints, which will include:

```
Package sagetex Warning: Graphics file
sage-plots-for-st_example.tex/plot-0.eps on page 1 does not exist. Plot
command is on input line 25.

Package sagetex Warning: There were undefined Sage formulas and/or
plots. Run Sage on st_example.sage, and then run LaTeX on
st_example.tex again.
```

Notice that, in addition to the usual collection of files produced by LaTeX, there is a file called `st_example.sage`. That is a Sage script produced when you run LaTeX on `st_example.tex`. The warning message told you to run Sage on `st_example.sage`, so take its advice and do that. It will tell you to run LaTeX on `st_example.tex` again, but before you do that, notice that a new file has been created: `st_example.sout`. That file contains the results of Sage's computations, in a format that LaTeX can use to insert into your text. A new directory containing an EPS file of your plot has also been created. Run LaTeX again and you'll see that everything that Sage computed and plotted is now included in your document.

The different macros used above should be pretty easy to understand. A `sageblock` environment typesets your code verbatim and also executes the code when you run Sage. When you do `\sage{foo}`, the result put into your document is whatever you get from running `latex(foo)` inside Sage. Plot commands are a bit more complicated, but in their simplest form, `\sageplot{foo}` inserts the image you get from doing `foo.save('filename.eps')`.

In general, the mantra is:

- run LaTeX on your .tex file;
- run Sage on the generated .sage file;
- run LaTeX again.

You can omit running Sage if you haven't changed around any Sage commands in your document.

There's a lot more to SageTeX, and since both Sage and LaTeX are complex, powerful tools, it's a good idea to read the documentation for SageTeX, which is in `SAGE_ROOT/local/share/texmf/tex/generic/sagetex`.

CHAPTER
EIGHT

AFTERWORD

8.1 Why Python?

8.1.1 Advantages of Python

The primary implementation language of Sage is Python (see [Py]), though code that must be fast is implemented in a compiled language. Python has several advantages:

- **Object saving** is well-supported in Python. There is extensive support in Python for saving (nearly) arbitrary objects to disk files or a database.

- Excellent support for **documentation** of functions and packages in the source code, including automatic extraction of documentation and automatic testing of all examples. The examples are automatically tested regularly and guaranteed to work as indicated.

- **Memory management**: Python now has a well thought out and robust memory manager and garbage collector that correctly deals with circular references, and allows for local variables in files.

- Python has **many packages** available now that might be of great interest to users of Sage: numerical analysis and linear algebra, 2D and 3D visualization, networking (for distributed computations and servers, e.g., via twisted), database support, etc.

- **Portability:** Python is easy to compile from source on most platforms in minutes.

- **Exception handling:** Python has a sophisticated and well thought out system of exception handling, whereby programs gracefully recover even if errors occur in code they call.

- **Debugger:** Python includes a debugger, so when code fails for some reason, the user can access an extensive stack trace, inspect the state of all relevant variables, and move up and down the stack.

- **Profiler:** There is a Python profiler, which runs code and creates a report detailing how many times and for how long each function was called.

- **A Language:** Instead of writing a **new language** for mathematics as was done for Magma, Maple, Mathematica, Matlab, GP/PARI, GAP, Macaulay 2, Simath, etc., we use the Python language, which is a popular computer language that is being actively developed and optimized by hundreds of skilled software engineers. Python is a major open-source success story with a mature development process (see [PyDev]).

8.1.2 The Pre-Parser: Differences between Sage and Python

Some mathematical aspects of Python can be confusing, so Sage behaves differently from Python in several ways.

- **Notation for exponentiation:** ** versus ^. In Python, ^ means "xor", not exponentiation, so in Python we have

```
>>> 2^8
10
>>> 3^2
1
>>> 3**2
9
```

This use of ^ may appear odd, and it is inefficient for pure math research, since the "exclusive or" function is rarely used. For convenience, Sage pre-parses all command lines before passing them to Python, replacing instances of ^ that are not in strings with **:

```
sage: 2^8
256
sage: 3^2
9
sage: "3^2"
'3^2'
```

The bitwise xor operator in Sage is ^^. This also works for the inplace operator ^^=:

```
sage: 3^^2
1
sage: a = 2
sage: a ^^= 8
sage: a
10
```

- **Integer division:** The Python expression 2/3 does not behave the way mathematicians might expect. In Python, if m and n are ints, then m/n is also an int, namely the quotient of m divided by n. Therefore 2/3=0. There has been talk in the Python community about changing Python so 2/3 returns the floating point number 0.6666..., and making 2//3 return 0.

We deal with this in the Sage interpreter, by wrapping integer literals in Integer( ) and making division a constructor for rational numbers. For example:

```
sage: 2/3
2/3
sage: (2/3).parent()
Rational Field
sage: 2//3
0
sage: int(2)/int(3)
0
```

- **Long integers:** Python has native support for arbitrary precision integers, in addition to C-int's. These are significantly slower than what GMP provides, and have the property that they print with an L at the end to distinguish them from int's (and this won't change any time soon). Sage implements arbitrary precision integers using the GMP C-library, and these print without an `L`.

Rather than modifying the Python interpreter (as some people have done for internal projects), we use the Python language exactly as is, and write a pre-parser for IPython so that the command line behavior of IPython is what a mathematician expects. This means any existing Python code can be used in Sage. However, one must still obey the standard Python rules when writing packages that will be imported into Sage.

(To install a Python library, for example that you have found on the Internet, follow the directions, but run `sage -python` instead of `python`. Very often this means typing `sage -python setup.py install`.)

8.2 I would like to contribute somehow. How can I?

If you would like to contribute to Sage, your help will be greatly appreciated! It can range from substantial code contributions to adding to the Sage documentation to reporting bugs.

Browse the Sage web page for information for developers; among other things, you can find a long list of Sage-related projects ordered by priority and category. The Sage Developer's Guide has helpful information, as well, and you can also check out the `sage-devel` Google group.

8.3 How do I reference Sage?

If you write a paper using Sage, please reference computations done with Sage by including

```
[Sage] William A. Stein et al., Sage Mathematics Software (Version 4.3).
       The Sage Development Team, 2009, http://www.sagemath.org.
```

in your bibliography (replacing 4.3 with the version of Sage you used). Moreover, please attempt to track down what components of Sage are used for your computation, e.g., PARI?, GAP?, Singular? Maxima? and also cite those systems. If you are in doubt about what software your computation uses, feel free to ask on the `sage-devel` Google group. See *Univariate Polynomials* for further discussion of this point.

If you happen to have just read straight through this tutorial, and have some sense of how long it took you, please let us know on the `sage-devel` Google group.

Have fun with Sage!

CHAPTER
NINE

APPENDIX

9.1 Arithmetical binary operator precedence

What is `3^2*4 + 2%5`? The value (38) is determined by this "operator precedence table". The table below is based on the table in § 5.14 of the *Python Language Reference Manual* by G. Rossum and F. Drake. the operations are listed here in increasing order of precedence.

Operators	Description
or	boolean or
and	boolean and
not	boolean not
in, not in	membership
is, is not	identity test
>, <=, >, >=, ==, !=	comparison
+, -	addition, subtraction
*, /, %	multiplication, division, remainder
**, ^	exponentiation

Therefore, to compute `3^2*4 + 2%5`, Sage brackets the computation this way: `((3^2)*4) + (2%5)`. Thus, first compute `3^2`, which is `9`, then compute both `(3^2)*4` and `2%5`, and finally add these.

105

CHAPTER TEN

BIBLIOGRAPHY

CHAPTER
ELEVEN

INDICES AND TABLES

- *genindex*
- *modindex*
- *search*

BIBLIOGRAPHY

[Cyt] Cython, http://www.cython.org.

[Dive] Dive into Python, Freely available online at http://diveintopython.org.

[GAP] The GAP Group, GAP - Groups, Algorithms, and Programming, Version 4.4; 2005, http://www.gap-system.org

[GAPkg] GAP Packages, http://www.gap-system.org/Packages/packages.html

[GP] PARI/GP http://pari.math.u-bordeaux.fr/.

[Ip] The IPython shell http://ipython.scipy.org.

[Jmol] Jmol: an open-source Java viewer for chemical structures in 3D http://www.jmol.org/.

[Mag] Magma http://magma.maths.usyd.edu.au/magma/.

[Max] Maxima http://maxima.sf.net/

[NagleEtAl2004] Nagle, Saff, and Snider. *Fundamentals of Differential Equations*. 6th edition, Addison-Wesley, 2004.

[Py] The Python language http://www.python.org/ Reference Manual http://docs.python.org/ref/ref.html.

[PyDev] Guido, Some Guys, and a Mailing List: How Python is Developed, http://www.python.org/dev/dev_intro.html.

[Pyr] Pyrex, http://www.cosc.canterbury.ac.nz/~greg/python/Pyrex/.

[PyT] The Python Tutorial http://www.python.org/.

[SA] Sage web site http://www.sagemath.org/.

[Si] G.-M. Greuel, G. Pfister, and H. Schönemann. Singular 3.0. A Computer Algebra System for Polynomial Computations. Center for Computer Algebra, University of Kaiserslautern (2005). http://www.singular.uni-kl.de.

[SJ] William Stein, David Joyner, Sage: System for Algebra and Geometry Experimentation, Comm. Computer Algebra {39}(2005)61-64.

Made in the USA
Middletown, DE
14 December 2016